SEAMLESS
PASTORAL
TRANSITION

SEAMLESS PASTORAL TRANSITION

3 Imperatives – 6 Pitfalls

LEE KRICHER

FOREWORD by CAREY NIEUWHOF

XULON PRESS

Xulon Press
2301 Lucien Way #415
Maitland, FL 32751
407.339.4217
www.xulonpress.com

All Scripture quotations, unless otherwise indicated,
are taken from The New Revised Standard Version
Updated Edition (NRSVUE)®

Paperback ISBN-13: 978-1-6628-5122-3
Ebook ISBN-13: 978-1-6628-5123-0

Table of Contents

Foreword vii

Introduction ix

Chapter 1   *Ancient Wisdom* 1

Chapter 2   *The First Imperative: Share Leadership* 17

Chapter 3   *The Second Imperative: Pave the Way* 35

Chapter 4   *The Third Imperative: Model Humility* 57

Chapter 5   *Leadership Transition Pitfalls* 83

Conclusion. 107

Works Cited 115

Foreword

Pastoral transition is reaching a crisis point in the Western church. And if you think succession is already a challenge, just give it a few years.

According to the Barna Group, the average senior pastor these days is in his or her late fifties. To make it more complicated, there isn't exactly a long line of next generation leaders cueing up to lead our churches. Which means if you're relying on external searches and more traditional methods of filling a vacancy, you could be waiting a long time.

That's why I'm so glad Lee Kricher has written this book. Having sat in the Senior Pastor seat myself as a Founding Pastor, I can underscore how critical it is to handle succession effectively. In our case, as in Lee's, it has led to the church becoming even stronger *after* succession than it was before.

As a former Lead Pastor committed to the next generation, here's what I know: there's no success without succession. If you build your church up only to have it fall apart or stumble after you leave, you'll have neglected one of your most important responsibilities.

Lee will help set up you and your team to create a succession strategy that will help your church thrive into the future. And who could want anything more than that?

Carey Nieuwhof
Bestselling Author, Speaker, and Founding Pastor of
Connexus Church

Introduction

I was perplexed when a pastor recently said to me, "I am responsible to lead my church while I am here. What happens after I am gone is not my issue." After investing decades of his life into the people of his church and community, this pastor was okay with the thought that his church could experience a steep decline once he leaves. He clearly doesn't get the point that author John Maxwell makes, "When all is said and done, your ability as a leader will not be judged by what you achieved personally or even by what your team accomplished during your tenure. You will be judged by how well your people and your organization did after you were gone."[1]

Dr. Jay Passavant did get the point. He is the founding pastor of North Way Christian Community. Founded in the early 1980s, North Way became the church home for thousands of members, who joined together to make a profound impact in their city and beyond. As he entered his sixties, it would have been easy for Jay to assume that he could and should lead the church indefinitely. After all, he was not lacking in passion. His leadership effectiveness showed no signs of decline. And yet he came to the prayerful conclusion that a pastoral transition to a next

---

[1] John Maxwell, *The 21 Irrefutable Laws of Leadership* (Nashville: Thomas Nelson, 2007), 249.

generation leader was the right choice for the ongoing health and vitality of North Way.

Pastor Jay worked hand in hand with a transition team commissioned by the church board of directors to determine the leader who would be most qualified to lead North Way into the future. Jay was sixty-four years old when the Seamless Pastoral Transition took place and his successor stepped into the role of Lead Pastor. Given the transparency of the process, the people of North Way Christian Community warmly welcomed the incoming pastor, whom they had come to know and respect as one of the Associate Pastors of the church. The positive momentum of North Way was not only maintained, it was accelerated.

I was deeply saddened in August 2021, when Pastor Jay Passavant died at age seventy-four. He had been diagnosed with cancer earlier that year, but no one expected such a sudden departure. Had he not led a Seamless Pastoral Transition at North Way several years earlier, his death would not just have been sad for the people of his congregation—it could have been devastating to the mission of North Way Christian Community. There is a long list of reasons why I believe that my friend left such an amazing legacy. His commitment to effective leadership transition is high on the list.

Seamless Pastoral Transition

Pastoral transitions are inevitable for every church. Unfortunately, pastoral transitions often result in a major setback for the church—and it is becoming increasingly difficult for churches to bounce back. One recent study that included 125,000 members from more than 900 churches showed that the average percentage of church members thinking about exploring other churches jumped from one percent per year to four percent per year when their current pastor left.

The common practice of hiring an interim pastor increased this instability. The study found that by the time the church had an interim pastor for six months, the average percentage of church members who were thinking about exploring other churches tripled from four percent to twelve percent a year.[2] The researcher notes, "Worship attendance isn't the only concern. By the time a church has had an interim pastor for six months or more, the typical church is reporting a net drop in revenue of seven percent per year. This is occurring at precisely the time when a church needs additional revenue to (a) fund a search process, (b) cover the costs of moving a pastor, (c) get the salary package of the pastor up-to-date, and (d) demonstrate to candidates that a church is on solid financial footing."[3] Few churches today can afford to experience such a loss in attendance, giving or overall congregational momentum.

One practice that can mitigate such setbacks is Seamless Pastoral Transition. While Seamless Pastoral Transition is not a new concept, it is an option that churches are choosing with increased frequency. *A Seamless Pastoral*

---

[2] J. Russel Crabtree, *Transition Apparitions: Why Much of What We Know About Pastoral Transitions is Wrong* (St. Louis: Magi Press, 2015), 46.

[3] Crabtree, *Transition Apparitions*, 47.

Transition is a leadership transition in which a pastoral vacancy is avoided by a planned overlap in service of the outgoing pastor and the incoming pastor. The outgoing pastor is involved in the selection of the incoming pastor, increasing the outgoing pastor's enthusiasm about their successor. The incoming pastor makes a meaningful relational connection with the outgoing pastor, increasing congregational stability because the incoming pastor builds on the foundation that has already been laid.

The benefits of a Seamless Pastoral Transition, when implemented with sound leadership transition principles, are significant. A Seamless Pastoral Transition ensures the continuity of a church's mission. It maintains a church's positive momentum. Just as important, a Seamless Pastoral Transition gives the congregation a priceless opportunity to observe godly leadership virtues in action as modeled by the outgoing and incoming pastors.

> A Seamless Pastoral Transition is a leadership transition in which a pastoral vacancy is avoided by a planned overlap in service of the outgoing pastor and the incoming pastor.

The Interim Model

Given the instability and loss of momentum that commonly occurs when churches are between permanent ("settled") pastors, it stands to reason that any gap in time between pastors would be considered highly undesirable. After all, the most effective for-profit and not-for-profit organizations are diligent about succession planning to avoid vacancies in key leadership positions. I know that in some situations a gap in time between permanent pastors is unplanned—a pastor unexpectedly leaves due to a physical or mental health crisis, marriage or family issues, moral failure, or some other reason unforeseen by those to whom the pastor is accountable. What is perplexing to me is that, in some churches, a gap in time between permanent pastors is actually *planned*. What I am referring to is the Interim Model.

The Interim Model, by design, *creates* a gap in time between permanent pastors. It commonly involves the appointment of an interim pastor, who serves for months or years before the next permanent pastor takes office. The Interim Model, which traces back to the 1970s[4], is based on the assumption that people in churches dealing with a pastoral transition need to experience healing before a new permanent pastor can take office. Carolyn Weese and J. Russel Crabtree write, "Today, one prevailing stream of thinking about leadership transition tends to be ill-ness-based. A pastoral departure is treated like a terminal diagnosis; just as no one plans for cancer, no one plans for a leadership transition either. Once the leader has moved, grief sets in. An entire body of literature has grown up around this illness-based approach to leadership

---

[4] Loren B. Mead, *Critical Moment of Ministry: A Change of Pastors* (Bethesda, MD: Alban Institute, 1986), 60.

transition."[5] Anthony B. Robinson points out, "Interim ministry, once an innovation, has now become the standard operating procedure, the 'one-size-fits-all' recourse for every church in pastoral transition when in fact one size doesn't fit all."[6] It is a flawed assumption that every church needs an interim period to find healing—or to find a "new identity"—when a pastor departs.

> It is a flawed assumption that every church needs an interim period to find healing—or to find a "new identity"—when a pastor departs.

Another flawed assumption behind the Interim Model is that churches can maintain their stability and momentum for months or even years between permanent pastors. As with many church practices, the Interim Model was established in a different world than exists today. There was a time when attending church was a social obligation. It was a time when people would commonly declare, "This is my church for life. It doesn't matter if I have a good pastor, a bad pastor, or no pastor. This is—and always will be—my church!" I grew up in such a church. In that predictable environment, the effectiveness and efficiency of the pastoral transition process were, at least to some degree, irrelevant to the viability of a church. So was the amount of time that passed between the departure of

---

[5] Carolyn Weese and J. Russell Crabtree, *The Elephant in the Board Room: Speaking the Unspoken About Pastoral Transitions* (San Francisco: Jossey-Bass, 2004), 19.

[6] Anthony B. Robinson, *Rethinking Interim Ministry*, (Chapel Hill: Alban Weekly, Alban at Duke Divinity School, January 9, 2013), 1.

one permanent pastor and the installation of the next. The idea that a church between pastors will continue to retain current members and attract new members is an idea based on the assumption that we still live in the good old days. We don't.

I recently spoke with a denominational leader who oversees pastoral transitions in United Presbyterian (PCUSA) churches. He indicated that the Interim Model has been over-idealized as a path for a congregation

> The idea that a church between pastors will continue to retain current members and attract new members is an idea based on the assumption that we still live in the good old days. We don't.

to find a new identity during the typical eighteen-month to two-year time period between permanent pastors. It is his conviction that alternatives need to be considered, with the well-being of each congregation becoming the highest priority. He said, "Necessity drives change. Instead of applying the Interim Model in every situation, we now approach things flexibly on a case-by-case basis." He spoke about three churches in his Presbytery that recently chose a Seamless Pastoral Transition, with the outgoing pastor and incoming pastor overlapping in their service. There was no interim period of time between permanent pastors. With the internal guidance of a pastoral nominating committee and the external support of the Presbytery, these congregations were able to maintain their vitality and ensure continuity of key ministries during the pastoral transition.

Considering New Approaches

In 2003, I was installed as Senior Pastor of Amplify Church. The church was in steep decline, as hundreds of regular attendees had vanished over the years. Of even greater concern was the fact that the average age of attendees was almost twenty years older than the average age of those in the community served by the church. It was heartwarming to hear from long-time church members about how God had used the church to positively impact their lives. It was heartbreaking to hear from the same people that their children and grandchildren would not attend church with them. We did not need to change our church beliefs or values, but we definitely needed to consider new approaches to church ministry. We made a number of changes and, over the next few years, we were blessed to witness the transformation of Amplify Church from an aging, dying church to a vibrant, multi-generational church.

I was moved to tears one Sunday morning when I spoke with Eleanor Evans, one of our church members in her late eighties. She indicated that she was not happy with a number of changes that had been initiated at the church, so I asked her, "Why do you keep coming and praying and giving, Eleanor?" She said, "Because now my children and my grandchildren will come to church with me. And I look around every week at the children and grandchildren of others who are filling our church. That means everything to me."[7]

---

[7] Lee Kricher, *For a New Generation: A Practical Guide for Revitalizing Your Church* (Grand Rapids: Zondervan, 2016), 124.

In a rapidly changing world, open-minded leaders in every type of organization, including churches, must consider new approaches. Entrepreneur and Author Seth Godin writes about the importance of re-calibrating, "What used to be smart is now dumb. What used to be risky is now the safe thing to do. We change. That's part of the deal. A well-lived life without calibration is unlikely."[8] It is not only wise, but necessary, for church leaders—pastors, denominational executives, and church board members—to re-calibrate their approach to many aspects of church life, including pastoral transitions. In her research into clergy supply in the twenty-first century, Patricia M.Y. Chang contends, "Some of the most fruitful exchanges of innovative ideas are likely to come from exchanges across denominations rather than within them."[9] Seamless Pastoral Transition, when coupled with sound principles of leadership transition, is one of those innovative ideas.

> In a rapidly changing world, open-minded leaders in every type of organization, including churches, must consider new approaches.

About This Book

This book contains several case studies of Seamless Pastoral Transitions that took place in churches from

---

[8] Seth Godin, *Seth's Blog,* March 28, 2022, https://seths.blog/2022/03/re-calibrating/

[9] Patricia M. Y. Chang, *Assessing the Clergy Supply in the 21st Century* (Durham: Duke Divinity School, 2004), 25.

various traditions including Anglican, Assemblies of God, Baptist, Christian and Missionary Alliance, Lutheran, Non-Denominational and United Methodist churches. I also write about the Seamless Pastoral Transition that took place at Amplify Church. It is interesting to note that Seamless Pastoral Transition is not typically practiced in some of these traditions, yet it still took place with the blessing of an open-minded bishop or other ecclesial authority overseeing the church.

I was privileged to personally interview leaders in each of the churches highlighted in this book. I observed that these churches, in which a Seamless Pastoral Transition took place, had one or more of the following characteristics:

- ✦ They were not in a significant crisis or in need of healing from a crisis.
- ✦ They were not struggling to find their identity or a renewed mission.
- ✦ They had a unique DNA and ministry in their community that congregation members did not want to risk being discontinued by an incoming pastor with a different vision.
- ✦ They were financially stable enough to pay both an outgoing pastor and incoming pastor during a period of time when they would both serve the church together, even if only for a few weeks.
- ✦ The outgoing pastor had served the congregation for many years and was loved and respected. (Fair or not, if the attitude of a congregation towards an

outgoing pastor is "good riddance," church members will have little interest in the outgoing pastor's endorsement of the incoming pastor.)

In general, these churches had "positive momentum" and were actively fulfilling their mission. While positive momentum cannot be defined merely in terms of attendance and/or giving, they definitely were not in steep decline or in danger of closing their doors.

Please note that the success of a Seamless Pastoral Transition is not measured by how well the church is doing in terms of attendance and giving years after the transition. There are too many variables involved with those metrics in any type of pastoral transition (i.e., a global pandemic). Nor is the word "seamless" interchangeable with the word "flawless." *The measure of success for a Seamless Pastoral Transition is simply that the health and momentum of a church are not negatively impacted by an unnecessary gap in time between permanent pastors.*

If you are convinced that a gap in time *is* needed between permanent pastors in the church(es) you serve, then this book is not for you. Much is written elsewhere about how to best implement the Interim Model, which has been used effectively in many situations. This book is written for church leaders who are open to the idea that a Seamless Pastoral

> *The measure of success for a Seamless Pastoral Transition is simply that the health and momentum of a church are not negatively impacted by an unnecessary gap in time between permanent pastors.*

Transition may be the right choice for their church. It focuses on three *Leadership Transition Imperatives* to embrace and covers six *Leadership Transition Pitfalls* to avoid. It includes insights, not only from the church case studies mentioned above, but also from biblical examples of seamless leadership transition and from the writings of leadership transition experts. Not all of those experts are church leaders, but I have found that God can teach us a lot when we don't restrict the sources of our learning.

I have spent portions of my career in the corporate world, the not-for-profit world, and the church world. The principles related to effective leadership succession and transition are, for the most part, universal. Yet, while I am passionate about the topic of leadership transition in general, I am particularly passionate about pastoral transition. Given our Christ-centered mission, leadership transitions in churches should be handled not just with sincere prayer, but also with great diligence. William Vanderbloemen and Warren Bird point out a powerful truth, "Few (pastors) are eager to admit that their time with their present church will one day end. Planning for that day of succession may be the biggest leadership task a leader and church will ever face. It may also be the most import-ant."[10] If you agree, please read on.

> Given our Christ-centered mission, leadership transitions in churches should be handled not just with sincere prayer, but also with great diligence.

---

[10] William Vanderbloemen and Warren Bird, *Next: Pastoral Succession That Works* (Grand Rapids: Baker, 2014), 9.

CHAPTER ONE

Ancient Wisdom

The topic of leadership transition in the early church is best studied without being confined to specific titles. As Carl Volz notes, "The New Testament has no exclusive form or terminology for ministry. Some churches have bishops and deacons, and others do not. Some have presbyters, while other ministers are called prophets, teachers, pastors, and evangelists (Eph. 4:11-12). Paul and Barnabus, referred to as apostles, are commissioned by prophets and teachers (Acts 13:1 ff.). The all-inclusive term which describes every gift of leadership is that of ministry (*diakonia*), but no single minister is universally recognized as holding primary authority."[11] While there is almost universal use of the term "pastor" as the leader of a local church today, this is not the case in the scriptures or in early church history. As a result, this chapter will focus on the broader topic of leadership transition.

In the days immediately following Pentecost, leaders seem to have been chosen with great unity of heart and mind. For instance, when a need arose for new leaders to support a ministry to widows, Peter and the apostles gathered a number of church members together and said, "'Therefore, brothers and sisters, select from among

---

[11] Carl A. Volz, "The Pastoral Office in the Early Church," *Word & World* 9, no. 4 (1989): 359.

yourselves seven men of good standing, full of the Spirit and of wisdom, whom we may appoint to this task, while we, for our part, will devote ourselves to prayer and to serving the word.' What they said pleased the whole community, and they chose Stephen, a man full of faith and the Holy Spirit, together with Philip, Prochorus, Nicanor, Timon, Parmenas, and Nicolaus, a proselyte of Antioch. They had these men stand before the apostles, who prayed and laid their hands on them." (Acts 6:3-6) The selection of Stephen and his colleagues by consensus was a beautiful example of community discernment.

Another example of community discernment is the unanimous selection of Paul and Barnabas as missionaries, which occurred when church leaders were worshipping and fasting. "Now in the church at Antioch there were prophets and teachers: Barnabas, Simeon who was called Niger, Lucius of Cyrene, Manaen a childhood friend of Herod the ruler, and Saul. While they were worshiping the Lord and fasting, the Holy Spirit said, 'Set apart for me Barnabas and Saul for the work to which I have called them.' Then after fasting and praying they laid their hands on them and sent them off." (Acts 13: 1-3) The leaders making these decisions were clearly led by the Holy Spirit.

Unfortunately, the difficulty of achieving Spirit-led consensus in selecting leaders is seen as early as the fifteenth chapter of Acts when Paul and Barnabas could not reach agreement on whether to take John Mark with them on their next journey. "The disagreement became so sharp that they parted company." (Acts 15:39) The inability of

Paul and Barnabus to reach agreement foreshadowed the difficulty that church leaders would have in reaching agreement on many topics in the centuries to come, including the selection of leaders. Everett Ferguson describes the selection of church leaders in the decades following Pentecost in this way; "The activity of the Spirit . . . gave way to other means of selection."[12]

John Chrysostom (347-407 C.E.), Archbishop of Constantinople, wrote about the chaos that was the norm during leadership transitions in his day: "Tell me, where do you think all the disorders in the church originate? I think their only origin is in the careless and random way in which the prelates are chosen and appointed."[13] He wrote:

> "The activity of the Spirit . . . gave way to other means of selection."

> Come and take a peep at the public festivals, at which it is the custom for most appointments to ecclesiastical office to be made. You will see the priest assailed with as many accusations as there are persons under his rule. For all who are qualified to bestow the honour are then split into many factions and the synod presbyters can be seen agreeing neither among themselves nor with the

[12] Everett Ferguson, *Ordination in the Ancient Church* (Restoration Quarterly 5 no. 3, 1961), 143.

[13] John Chrysostom, *Six Books on the Priesthood* (Crestwood, NY: St. Vladimir's Seminary Press, 1996), 79.

one who has received the episcopal office. Each man stands alone. One chooses this candidate and another that. The reason is that they do not all concentrate on the one thing they should – spiritual worth. There are other considerations which influence appointments to office. For example, one man says "Let this man be chosen, because he belongs to a distinguished family"; another says, "Because he possesses a large fortune and would not need supporting out of the Church's revenues; another, "Because he is a convert from the other side." One man is anxious to promote above the rest a friend, another a relative, another someone who flatters him. No one will look for the best qualified man.[14]

John Chrysostom's observations would indicate that the process of selecting church leaders at the time would hardly be described as being led by the Holy Spirit. His observations also indicate that leadership transitions in the Church have never been easy.

Two practices related to effective leadership transition can be observed in early church history, at least anecdotally. One of those practices is the involvement of outgoing leaders in the choice of their successors. Neil McLynn writes about Ambrose (c. 339 – c. 397) when he approached the

---

[14] John Chrysostom, *Six Books on the Priesthood*, 89.

end of his tenure as Bishop of Milan, "Ambrose retained his authority until the very end. So instinctive was it for his disciples to find oracular significance in the bishop's every word that an exclamation from his sickbed, duly interpreted, secured the nomination of the venerable Simplicianus as his successor.[15] Augustine (c. 354 – c. 430) also chose his successor. According to Martin Bucer, "Among the epistles of St Augustine we have the records of the election and appointment of Eradius, whom St Augustine chose and appointed to be his successor."[16] Succession planning in the Church is not a particularly new or novel idea.

Another practice that can be observed in early church history is the commitment to fill pastoral vacancies quickly, if not immediately. In 1527, leaders of the Free Church (Brotherhood Church) met in Schleitheim, Switzerland. Those gathered agreed on seven points of faith, including a process for appointing new pastors. According to the *Schleitheim Confession*, "We have been united as follows concerning shepherds in the church of God. . . if the shepherd should be driven away or led to the Lord by the cross, at the same hour another shall be ordained to his place, so that the little folk and the little flock may not be destroyed, but be preserved by warning and be consoled."[17] At the time,

---

[15] Neil B. McLynn, *Ambrose of Milan* (Berkeley: University of California Press, 1994), 367.

[16] Martin Bucer. *Concerning the True Care of Souls* (Edinburgh, UK: The Banner of Truth Trust, 2009), 64.

[17] John Yoder, *The Schleitheim Confession* (Scottdale, PA: Herald Press, 1977), 13-14.

these churches were enduring extreme persecution, and it was not unusual for local pastors to be "led to the Lord by the cross," indicating martyrdom. In such a situation, a pastoral successor was to be named "at the same hour." Like succession planning, preserving continuity of church leadership by avoiding a gap in time between leaders is not a particularly new or novel idea.

Moses and Joshua

Succession planning and preserving continuity of leadership are both evident in the most extensive biblical record of leadership transition—the account of the transition from Moses to Joshua. Several principles emerge when this leadership transition is studied, including insights from this passage:

> Then Moses summoned Joshua and said to him in the sight of all Israel, "Be strong and bold, for you are the one who will go with this people into the land that the Lord has sworn to their ancestors to give them, and you will put them in possession of it. It is the Lord who goes before you. He will be with you; he will not fail you or forsake you. Do not fear or be dismayed." (Deuteronomy 31:7-8)

First, the leadership transition from Moses to Joshua was *planned*. Moses clearly felt that he had a God-given responsibility to identify the leader who would take his place. Though there were other effective leaders in the nation of Israel, Moses "summoned" Joshua. There is a critical question that every leader must ask—"Am I responsible for what happens after I leave my leadership role?" Moses would have answered that question in the affirmative. He could not guarantee what would happen to the nation of Israel after his death, but he could make sure that the people were left with a proven, effective leader.

> There is a critical question that every leader must ask—"Am I responsible for what happens after I leave my leadership role?" Moses would have answered that question in the affirmative.

Second, the leadership transition was *transparent*. The people of Israel were not left in the dark about who would lead them when Moses was gone. The appointment of Joshua by Moses was done "in the sight of all Israel" (v.7). Joshua did not have to convince Israel after Moses was gone that he had been chosen in private by Moses. Those most affected by the leadership transition were eyewitnesses as Moses commissioned Joshua as their next leader.

Finally, the leadership transition was *seamless*. This was a deliberate choice on the part of Moses, who chose Joshua to take over the leadership of Israel in a transition that would involve no gap in time between the leaders. Joshua's leadership began the moment Moses' leadership ended. Moses clearly

> Joshua's leadership began the moment Moses' leadership ended. Moses clearly believed that a seamless leadership transition was God's will and in the best interests of God's people.

believed that a seamless leadership transition was God's will and in the best interests of God's people.

Brent Strawn does not see the leadership transition from Moses to Joshua merely in terms of providing Israel with a new national and military leader, but as providing the nation with a new "scribe-king" and "designated reader of the Law" who would ensure continuity of Israel's connection to God. He writes, "Deuteronomy's scribe-king functions as something akin to Israel's 'pastor'—one tasked with the community's instruction in the language of faith— and the model of the designated reader becomes a pregnant one for contemporary ministers."[18] Strawn's use of the word "pastor" to describe the roles of Moses and Joshua is provocative. Christian leaders who have the conviction that Seamless Pastoral Transition is in the best interest of a given church have much to learn from the planned, transparent, seamless leadership transition from "Pastor" Moses to "Pastor" Joshua. Three virtues are evident in their leadership transition—Sharing Leadership, Paving the Way, and Modeling Humility.

Moses Shared Leadership

Knowing how God had revealed himself to him and used him, Moses seemed to have embraced a *One Leader— Many Followers* paradigm, a leadership paradigm in which all meaningful leadership is built around a central leader. That is understandable. He was the catalyst for the miracles

---

[18] Brent A. Strawn, *The Old Testament is Dying: A Diagnosis and Recommended Treatment* (Grand Rapids: Baker Academic, 2017), 200.

that led to the stunning release of the Jewish people from slavery in Egypt. God had used him to part the Red Sea and receive the Ten Commandments. He didn't seem to feel an urgency to develop other leaders since, after all, he was "the man."

That all changed when he got a visit from his father-in-law, Jethro. Not long after the exodus from Egypt, Jethro visited Moses and was delighted to hear about the amazing things that God had done through Moses for Israel. Jethro then spent a day with Moses observing his leadership in action. "The next day Moses sat as judge for the people, while the people stood around him from morning until evening. When Moses's father-in-law saw all that he was doing for the people, he said, 'What is this that you are doing for the people? Why do you sit alone, while all the people stand around you from morning until evening?' Moses said to his father-in-law, 'Because the people come to me to inquire of God. When they have a dispute, they come to me, and I decide between one person and another, and I make known to them the statutes and instructions of God.' Moses's father-in-law said to him, 'What you are doing is not good.'" (Exodus 18:13-17)

Moses likely had a relatively close relationship with Jethro. After all, Moses worked for him and with him for several decades in Midian. Still, it is hard to imagine what was going on in Moses' mind when his father-in-law uttered those words, "What you are doing is not good." Moses could have easily responded defensively, "Jethro, I am not the guy you knew in Midian. Since that time, I led this entire nation out of slavery in Egypt. The Red Sea parted when I lifted my staff. I have an inside track to God like no one else on the planet. Are you sure you feel a need to critique my leadership?" But no matter how Moses was feeling about it, he listened to Jethro's advice. He began to share meaningful leadership with others, appointing judges to resolve the vast majority of Israel's issues. (Exodus 18:18-26) While Moses did not abdicate his role as Israel's leader, he gave many others opportunities to lead.

Two outstanding leaders that Moses identified and trusted as leaders were Caleb and Joshua. Joshua led a militia group to fight the Amalekites. Moses took Joshua with him for at least a portion of his first ascent to and descent from Mount Sinai. Moses chose Joshua and Caleb as two of the twelve men who scouted out the land of Canaan. In short, Moses came to understand the need to intentionally elevate others to take on visible leadership roles that supplemented his leadership role. Moses exchanged the *One Leader—Many Followers* paradigm for a commitment to identify and develop many leaders—and share leadership in a meaningful way. When it was time for Moses to hand off his leadership role in Israel, Joshua emerged from among many proven leaders of Israel.

> Moses came to understand the need to intentionally elevate others to take on visible leadership roles that supplemented his leadership role.

Moses Paved the Way for Joshua

Moses heard God's voice many times in his life, but we do not see his choice of a successor being determined by the kind of dramatic experience he had when he heard God's voice from the burning bush. God simply told Moses to "charge Joshua and encourage and strengthen him, because it is he who shall cross over at the head of this people and who shall secure their possession of the land that you will see." (Deuteronomy 3:28) Did Moses resist God's choice of Joshua? No. Moses was known to argue with God from time to time, but this was not one of those times. One reason may have been because Moses had already seen Joshua's leadership in action.

Moses witnessed Joshua's courage and faith when Joshua returned from scouting out the promised land. Ten of the twelve men whom Moses appointed to report about what they observed in the land of Canaan instilled fear in the people of Israel by delivering a bad report: "The land that we have gone through as spies is a land that devours its inhabitants, and all the people that we saw in it are of great size…To ourselves we seemed like grasshoppers, and so we seemed to them." (Numbers 13: 32-33). Joshua took exception to their doubts and fears and encouraged the people to trust in God.

Interestingly enough, Joshua was not the only one to show extraordinary leadership at that critical moment. We read, "Caleb quieted the people before Moses and said, 'Let us go up at once and occupy it, for we are well able to over-come it.'" (Numbers 13:30). When the people continued to express fear and unbelief, Caleb declared, "The land that we went through as spies is an exceedingly good land. If the Lord is pleased with us, he will bring us into this land and give it to us, a land that flows with milk and honey. Only, do not rebel against the Lord." (Numbers 14:7-9) Given the leadership and courage demonstrated here by Caleb, it is no surprise that God spoke to Moses that Caleb was a man with a "different spirit" who followed God wholeheartedly. (Numbers 14:24). When considering Caleb, who stayed faithful to God for decades to come, it is clear that Joshua was not the only proven leader whom Moses could have chosen as his successor. Moses prayerfully chose Joshua from among many capable leaders in Israel.

Moses paved the way for Joshua's future leadership role by providing him with highly visible leadership opportunities. By the time Joshua was commissioned as the leader of the nation of Israel, he was already established as a credible and respected leader. According to Haubert and Clinton, "Joshua's ongoing association with Moses at a mentoring level did at least two things. First, it promoted Joshua's development. Through tandem training Joshua was inculcating skills, attitudes and values needed for top level leadership. Second, it prepared the people for Joshua's installation. Whenever they saw Moses, Joshua was not far away. This gave Joshua credibility and created a positive perception of his status."[19]

---

[19] Kathrine Haubert and Bobby Clinton, *The Joshua Portrait: A Study in Leadership Development, Leadership Transition, & Destiny Fulfillment* (Altadena, CA: Barnabas Publishers, 1990), 79.

Moses also paved the way for Joshua by making sure that the leadership transition was simple, straightforward and very public. "Then Moses summoned Joshua and said to him in the sight of all Israel, "Be strong and bold, for you are the one who will go with this people into the land that the Lord has sworn to their ancestors to give them, and you will put them in possession of it. It is the Lord who goes before you. He will be with you; he will not fail you or forsake you. Do not fear or be dismayed." (Deuteronomy 31:7-8) For years, Moses had empowered Joshua with leadership opportunities in the nation of Israel. His clear and unwavering support for Joshua paved the way for Joshua's success in leading Israel into the promised land of Canaan.

> For years, Moses had empowered Joshua with leadership opportunities in the nation of Israel. His clear and unwavering support for Joshua paved the way for Joshua's success in leading Israel into the promised land of Canaan.

Moses and Joshua Modeled Humility

The clear and unwavering support that Moses showed for Joshua certainly required humility on the part of Moses. It would have been understandable for Moses to deem himself to be irreplaceable. In fact, if any leader could have viewed himself as an "indispensable hero," it would have been Moses. Instead, Moses modeled the critical virtue of humility. According to Numbers 12:3, "Now the man Moses was very humble, more so than anyone else on the face of the earth." I have to admit that when I first read this

13

passage as a college student who held the view that the book of Numbers was written by the hand of Moses, the cynical thought crossed my mind that if Moses recorded the fact that he was the most humble person on earth, maybe he wasn't so humble after all. Despite such cynicism, it is safe to conclude from this passage that Moses was a leader who modeled humility.

But this critical leadership virtue of humility was not just demonstrated by Moses, it was also demonstrated by Joshua. Joshua showed clear and unwavering support and respect for Moses. Joshua did not start his tenure as Israel's leader by declaring, "Now that Moses is finally gone, I will take over and things are going to be really different now!" He did not introduce his own version of the Ten Commandments. Instead, he looked to the future by building on and honoring the past. Derek Tidball commends Joshua, noting, "Some leaders are naively eager to move people on from their present, somewhat settled position, and think the only way to do so is to write off the past, reject completely what's gone before and eradicate previous leaders from the story they want to create."[20] Tidball goes on to point out, "Leaders can be so keen to move on to a new age that they ignore the work done by their predecessor (or predecessors) on which they are building. Others may feel that their predecessors messed up or stayed past the point of effectiveness, and so maintain a noticeable

---

[20] Derek Tidball. *Lead Like Joshua: Lessons For Today* (London: InterVarsity Press, 2017), 7.

silence about them, which achieves nothing except to feed suspicions or erode loyalties."[21]

There were many instances when leaders in Israel dishonored Moses. Aaron dishonored Moses by allowing the people of Israel to worship an idol while Moses was on Mount Sinai. Miriam openly questioned Moses' judgment in his choice of a wife. In Numbers 16, we read about the open rebellion of Korah against Moses. Joshua would have witnessed firsthand that such dishonor led to unwanted outcomes—not the least of which was the opening of the earth to swallow up Korah and his friends.

Having witnessed how things turned out when other leaders dishonored Moses, Joshua wisely chose a different path. Even though Moses was not a perfect person, there is no record of Joshua ever criticizing or undermining the leadership of Moses. On the contrary, he honored Moses from the time of the exodus from Egypt to the day that Joshua died. We never even see him expressing impatience about how long he had to wait to take over Moses' role.

Given that Moses and Joshua both modeled humility in how they honored one another, it is no wonder that the people of Israel who loved and respected Moses showed the same love and respect for Joshua. "They answered Joshua: 'All that you have commanded us we will do,

> Given that Moses and Joshua both modeled humility in how they honored one another, it is no wonder that the people of Israel who loved and respected Moses showed the same love and respect for Joshua.

---

[21] Derek Tidball. *Lead Like Joshua*, 137.

and wherever you send us we will go. Just as we obeyed Moses in all things, so we will obey you'" (Joshua 1:16-17). The way that Moses and Joshua humbly honored one another clearly had a significant impact on their successful seamless leadership transition.

The transition from Moses to Joshua is not the only seamless leadership transition found in scripture, but the record of that transition is more extensive than any other. There are many insights that can be drawn from the biblical record of their leadership transition, including the timeless virtues of sharing leadership, paving the way, and modeling humility that they demonstrated—virtues that can be instructive to leaders in transition today. I think of the virtues demonstrated by Moses and Joshua as *Leadership Transition Imperatives*.

The chapters that follow contain accounts of leaders who were involved in a Seamless Pastoral Transition. In each situation, prayer was the foundation. Acknowledging dependence on God's guidance and favor was the most important factor in each pastoral transition. But these leaders also attribute their success, at least in part, to one or more of these *Leadership Transition Imperatives*: Share Leadership. Pave the Way. Model Humility.

CHAPTER TWO

The First Imperative:
Share Leadership

Jeff Henderson worked in Chick-fil-A's marketing department for six years. He became a fan of many things about Chick-fil-A, especially its culture. He better understood how that culture was created during a road trip with Chick-fil-A founder Truett Cathy. Rather than talking business, Mr. Cathy asked about Jeff's family. He asked about Jeff's life. The questions were not surface, and Mr. Cathy listened with genuine interest. For Jeff, the conversation created an unforgettable memory. His conclusion speaks volumes about Chick-fil-A's culture; "Truett was more interested in the business growing people than he was in people growing the business. And that's exactly how his business grew."[22]

Since it was founded in 1946, Chick-fil-A has grown from a single restaurant serving hundreds of people to thousands of restaurants serving millions of people. I personally had the opportunity to see how leaders operated at

> "Truett was more interested in the business growing people than he was in people growing the business. And that's exactly how his business grew."

---

[22] Jeff Henderson, *Know What You're FOR: A Growth Strategy for Work, An Even Better Strategy for Life.* (Grand Rapids: Zondervan, 2019), 23.

Chick-fil-A during the years I lived in Atlanta, serving in the role of a leadership consultant. The Chick-fil-A leaders I spent time with were sincere people who led out of deeply held core values. One of those core values is a deep commitment to leadership development—a commitment that results in identifying emerging leaders and giving them meaningful leadership opportunities. Mark Miller, Vice President of High Performing Leadership at Chick-fil-A, was a recent guest on the Carey Nieuwhof Leadership Podcast. Mark shared, "There's something every organization needs more than leadership; they need a leadership culture. And that's a place where leaders are routinely and systematically developed and you have a surplus."

Given this commitment to leadership development and shared leadership, it is no surprise that seamless leadership transitions are the norm at Chick-fil-A. At the CEO level, a seamless leadership transition occurred in 2013 when Truett Cathy handed off his role to his son, Dan Cathy. Another seamless leadership transition occurred in 2021 when Dan Cathy handed off his role to his son, Andrew Cathy. According to Dan Cathy, "While rare in business today, deliberate, long-term succession planning provides us with stability and continuity at a time of tremendous opportunity."[23]

What is fascinating is that seamless leadership transitions are not just practiced at the highest level, but throughout the organization. CFO Brent Ragsdale explains,

---

[23] Ben Warren, *Chick-fil-A CEO Dan Cathy Steps Down* (Chicago: Mainland, 1851 Franchise, 09/17/21)

"Chick-fil-A is highly focused on succession planning and intentional about career pathing." It is no surprise, then, that Chick-fil-A provides organization-wide development of current and future leaders. Ragsdale's advice for leaders in any organization is clear and compelling: "Make sure you have at least one leader in mind that can step into your role at any time….It is crucial to constantly develop leaders."[24]

In addition to intentional leadership development, there is another fascinating concept that emerges from the most recent seamless leadership transition of Chick-fil-A's CEOs. Dan Cathy transitioned his role when he was still at the top of his game. Under his leadership, Chick-fil-A's revenue grew from $1 billion to $16 billion. As he discussed his leadership transition, Dan told Chick-fil-A operators and staff, "I'm in excellent health. I continue to love this business and all of you with all my heart, and I'm as energized as I've ever been about Chick-fil-A and our shared future."[25] Why, then would he hand off his leadership role? His explanation is striking. Most senior leaders think about leadership transition with one thing in mind— "When do I feel that I am ready?" Dan Cathy explained, "The most successful CEO transitions are made when the

> Most senior leaders think about leadership transition with one thing in mind— "When do I feel that I am ready?"

---

[24] Krystina Colyer, *Finance Team Building & Succession Planning Program Summary* (CFO Forum, August 6, 2019) 6-8.

[25] Joel Crews, *Chick-fil-A Names Next CEO* (Kansas City: SOSLAND Publishing, MEAT+POULTRY, 9-17-2021)

next leader is ready to lead."[26] The timing of this leadership transition was not driven by when the outgoing leader felt that he was ready, but rather when the incoming leader was ready!

Senior leaders in any type of organization can learn much from the seamless leadership transitions that take place at Chick-fil-A. It is about what is best for the organization, not just what is best for the outgoing leader. It is also about being passionate about shared leadership.

Unfortunately, shared leadership can be observed in the corporate world more readily than in the church world. There are many responsibilities that pastors readily accept, including overseeing church services and ministries, managing church staff and volunteers, and making sure that pastoral care is provided for church members. Most pastors are living examples of the passage, "Tend the flock of God that is in your charge, exercising the oversight, not under compulsion but willingly, as God would have you do it—not for sordid gain but eagerly." (1 Peter 5:2) And yet developing leaders and sharing leadership are not always priorities for pastors—perhaps because leadership development is not a topic commonly covered in many seminaries.

Researcher David Kinnaman points out, "We are nearing a critical juncture in church leadership. As the average age of pastors increases, there is growing concern about the need to identify and develop a new generation of leaders. If you are a pastor, no matter your age or tenure

---

[26] Ben Warren, *Chick-fil-A CEO Dan Cathy Steps Down* (Chicago: Mainland,1851 Franchise, 09/17/21)

at your current church, it's time to think about future leadership. Make mentoring tomorrow's church leaders a priority of your own ministry."[27] Many church leaders, though, have adopted the *One Leader—Many Followers* paradigm. In this approach to ministry, the pastor is accountable for recruiting volunteers and assigning tasks to staff members, but not for identifying and developing leaders. One pastor told me he gave up trying to develop leaders when a board member told him, "We are paying you to be the leader. We are not paying you to try and find others so you can dump your responsibilities." Clearly this board member embraced the *One Leader—Many Followers* paradigm for his pastor.

Another pastor I spoke with was not discouraged by a board member from developing leaders. He noted, "If I had any staff members or volunteers in my church with real leadership potential, I would consider leadership development a priority. I don't." His attitude about the leadership potential of the people in his church was similar to Jesse's attitude about the leadership potential of his son, David. He just didn't see it. That is until the prophet Samuel forced him to see it. Unfortunately, most pastors don't have a Samuel to open their eyes to the Davids in their churches.

Perhaps the most troubling reason some pastors don't develop leaders is that the *One Leader—Many Followers* paradigm plays to their self-esteem. One pastor

> Unfortunately, most pastors don't have a Samuel to open their eyes to the Davids in their churches.

---

[27] David Kinnaman, *Leadership Transitions: How Churches Navigate Pastoral Change – and Stay Healthy* (Grand Rapids: Baker, 2019), 7, 100-101.

I knew well did a great job growing his church and endearing himself to the congregation. He was highly honored. When he left without warning to pastor a larger church, the congregation was stunned. There were no other leadership voices to encourage them and the church went into rapid decline.

In his classic book, *The Leadership Engine*, Noel Tichy writes, "A person may have all the other traits of leadership, but if he or she doesn't personally see to the development of new leaders, the organization won't be sustainable, and the person is not a true leader—or at least not a winning one. If you look across history and across all fields of endeavor, you will see that this is true. Institutions and movements succeed over the long term...because they continually regenerate leadership at all levels. Jesus, Gandhi, and Martin Luther King Jr. all understood this. They all had strong ideas, values, energy and edge, but without disciples to spread their mission, both during their lifetimes and after their deaths, their legacies would have been short-lived."[28] Pastors who are

> "A person may have all the other traits of leadership, but if he or she doesn't personally see to the development of new leaders, the organization won't be sustainable, and the person is not a true leader."

> Pastors who are passionate about what will happen in their church when their tenure ends need to make developing leaders and sharing leadership high priorities.

---

[28] Noel M. Tichy, *The Leadership Engine: How Winning Companies Build Leaders at Every Level* (New York: HarperCollins, 1997), 42-43.

passionate about what will happen in their church when their tenure ends need to make developing leaders and sharing leadership high priorities.

Shared Leadership at Charter Oak Church

Charter Oak Church is a United Methodist Church that was one of the fastest growing churches in the community, with an average weekly attendance of approximately 500 people. According to the outgoing pastor, the growth was sparked by the vision "to reach out to those who are searching and equip believers to be fully devoted followers of Jesus." Knowing that his time of service at Charter Oak was coming to an end, the Lead Pastor chose Seamless Pastoral Transition—primarily to ensure that the momentum and continuity of the church would be maintained.

However, there was a major problem. Outgoing pastors in the United Methodist Church are not involved in the selection of incoming pastors. The norm is for a denominational executive to lead the process of replacing the outgoing pastor in partnership with the church council. Yet after much prayer, the outgoing pastor felt that a Seamless Pastoral Transition was right for Charter Oak. He talked about it with the Bishop who provided oversight for Charter Oak Church. The Bishop was open to the idea and he worked with the outgoing pastor to create a plan that would culminate in Charter Oak's Associate Pastor taking on the role of

> Even though Seamless Pastoral Transition was not the norm in his denomination, the Bishop declared, "Let's see what God does."

Lead Pastor. Even though Seamless Pastoral Transition was not the norm in his denomination, the Bishop declared, "Let's see what God does."

After working together to create a three-year formal leadership transition plan, the outgoing pastor and incoming pastor met several times each week to ensure that they were on the same page about the transition. After being approved by the church council, the transition plan was shared with transparency with the staff and congregation. There was a significant commitment to "over-communicate" about the upcoming Seamless Pastoral Transition.

There was an equally significant commitment demonstrated by the outgoing pastor to share leadership. In the year before the formal handoff, the incoming pastor spoke at half of the Sunday worship services and was involved in every staff and council decision. The obvious support that the beloved outgoing pastor had for the incoming pastor led to the overwhelming support of the congregation for their new Lead Pastor.

As with the outgoing pastor, the incoming pastor had a deep-seated passion for sharing leadership. The incoming pastor focused on identifying and developing potential leaders in the church—both staff and volunteers. He turned loose these emerging leaders to play key leadership roles in various areas of the church. Charter Oak entered a new season of health and growth with weekend church attendance growing to more than 1,500 people.

Shared Leadership at North Way Christian Community

North Way Christian Community is a non-denominational church that was founded in the early 1980s. In this book's Introduction, I refer to the founding pastor of North Way, Dr. Jay Passavant. From the start, Jay was convinced that he had a God-given responsibility to identify and develop leaders at North Way. It was a priority throughout his thirty-year tenure at the church. He was committed, as he put it, to "turn people loose." It made a difference. By 2011, the church had grown to 4,000 members attending one of several campuses.

Leaders were given significant roles in various areas of ministry throughout North Way. They were also given the encouragement and budget to grow in their leadership effectiveness through formal and informal development opportunities. As a result, the church developed an outstanding "pipeline" of leaders. Giving room for leaders to grow and serve made North Way a place where excellent leaders were attracted and retained. It made it possible for North Way to be one of the most impactful churches in the region.

As he entered his sixties, Jay Passavant came to the prayerful conclusion that a Seamless Pastoral Transition to a next generation leader was best for North Way. He then had to identify who that leader would be. Many leaders in his situation would have engaged the services of a national firm to conduct an external search to find the "perfect" leader to lead North Way Christian Community into its next season of ministry. However, because Pastor Jay had been so committed to developing leaders, there were numerous internal candidates who had demonstrated extraordinary leadership skills. They were already passionate about the mission of North Way. They were already champions of the culture of North Way. Though they had leadership gifts and styles that differed from one another's and Jay's, they were already proven leaders.

Instead of hiring a search firm, Jay hired a highly respected leadership assessment firm. Four of the most effective leaders at North Way Christian Community went through a rigorous and thorough leadership assessment process. Given the results of that assessment, he worked hand in hand with a transition team commissioned by the church board of directors to determine the leader who would be most qualified and prepared to lead North Way into the future. Jay was sixty-four years old when the Seamless Pastoral Transition took place and his successor stepped into the role of Senior Pastor.

Given the transparency of the process, the people of North Way Christian Community warmly welcomed the incoming pastor—whom they already knew and loved. The positive momentum of North Way was not only maintained, it was accelerated. Interestingly, the incoming pastor, who had experienced firsthand the positive impact of Seamless Pastoral Transition, handed off the Senior Pastor role to his successor eleven years later. Once again, the positive momentum of the church was not only maintained, but accelerated.

There were many factors involved in both of the Seamless Pastoral Transitions at North Way, but there is no doubt that one key factor was the ongoing commitment to identify and develop leaders. The most recent incoming pastor puts it this way, "Leadership development is at the top of my job description because the speed of leadership development determines how much we can grow. That is why a key to my assessment of leaders at North Way is directly tied to their success at developing other leaders."

> "Leadership development is at the top of my job description because the speed of leadership development determines how much we can grow."

Shared Leadership at Amplify Church

Amplify Church is the non-denominational church that I had the privilege to pastor twice, first in its early years from 1976-1990 and then again from 2003-2019. During my early years of pastoral ministry, developing other leaders was not a priority. I was a very different kind of pastor during my second tenure as pastor, to a great degree because of what I had learned during my years outside of ministry working in the corporate world. We had a noble goal—to make sure that the mission of the church would never be compromised due to a lack of ready leaders. A few foundational principles shaped our approach to shared leadership:

> We had a noble goal—to make sure that the mission of the church would never be compromised due to a lack of ready leaders.

+ *The primary role of every leader is to develop other leaders.* Leaders at Amplify did not just make sure that their responsibilities were fulfilled with excellence, they were also committed to mentoring others to do the same. I pro-actively served as a mentor to a number of potential leaders in our church, including the person who eventually became my successor. But mentoring was not just my responsibility. Every leader at Amplify Church committed to mentoring at least two people who could effectively carry out each of their key roles. That allowed us to be "three-deep" (the leader plus the two people being mentored) at every key role in the church. We built a mentoring culture by making it clear that leadership effectiveness is best demonstrated when the leader is not present. I was so pleased to hear one of our church staff members say, "We exist to pull the gold out of people so they can fulfill their purpose."

> The primary role of every leader is to develop other leaders.

+ *The leaders of tomorrow are already here.* Rather than assuming that we needed to hire new leaders from outside of Amplify Church, we assumed that future leaders would emerge from those who attended the church. Every leader was engaged in "shoulder-tapping," inviting new potential leaders to unearth and develop their God-given potential. It was common for volunteers to become part-time staff members and for part-time staff members to become full-time staff members. We paid for potential leaders to get the education and training they needed, including paying for advanced degrees for several staff members. In fact, we set approximately two percent of the church budget aside for professional development. The benefits of this approach compared with hiring externally were significant. We never had a question about the individual's passion for the vision of the church. They had already bought into the vision. We never had a question about the individual's respect for those in church leadership. They had already been following the lead of those in positions of authority in the church. We never had a question about the individual's sincerity and faithfulness. It had already been proven.

♦ *Leaders grow while doing.* While leaders can learn valuable truths through many avenues, they learn best when in action. That is why "shadowing" current leaders is the primary way we developed future leaders. After watching and experiencing how a current leader fulfilled their role, future leaders tried it themselves with the support and coaching of the current leader. Positive feedback coupled with feedback for improvement prepared the future leader for excellence in fulfilling their roles—and modeled for them how they would help to develop other leaders. By the way, shying away from feedback for improvement helps no one. John Maxwell writes, "When a person's behavior is inappropriate, *avoiding confrontation always worsens the situation.* First, the organization suffers because the person is not acting in its best interest. Second, you suffer because the person's deficiencies reduce your effectiveness. And finally, when a person is acting inappropriately and isn't told, you have robbed him of an important opportunity to learn and grow in his development process."[29] We made providing timely, specific feedback to Amplify Church's emerging leaders a high priority. It is a gift that accelerated leadership growth, effectiveness and impact.

With these foundational principles in place, we intentionally placed emerging leaders in visible leadership roles—often before some people thought they were ready. Of course, placing proven, established leaders in key leadership roles is safer. Giving unproven leaders a platform comes with risks. Some of the leaders we empowered disappointed us. Most did not. We found that giving next generation leaders significant and visible leadership responsibilities was an important part of the equation when it came to shared leadership and developing a pipeline of leaders.

---

[29] John Maxwell, *Developing the Leaders Around You: How to Help Others Reach Their Full Potential* (New York: HarperCollins Leadership,1995), 121.

For Reflection

When I first read the parable of Jesus in Matthew 25:14-30 about the responses of those who were given various talents, I knew that I had to identify and use my gifts (monetary and non-monetary) to fulfill God's purpose in my life. After all, the only person in the parable who did not hear the words, "Well done, good and faithful servant" was the person who buried his talents. At some point, though, I became convinced that, as a leader, I had to do more. I came to believe that it is not enough for me to unearth my talents, I also must help those in my sphere of influence to unearth their talents. As leadership guru Peter Drucker puts it, "The fruit of your labor grows on other people's trees."[30]

> It is not enough for me to unearth my talents, I also must help those in my sphere of influence to unearth their talents.

Had Jesus not shared leadership, first with His twelve closest disciples and then with many more, what would have happened after His death, resurrection and ascension? Lorin Woolfe writes, "It was no accident that this carefully picked group of twelve men was soon able to develop many times that number of leaders to spread the message and power the organization. Once 'the Twelve' became 'the Seventy-Two,' an inexorable process was set in motion."[31]

---

[30] Dean Niewolny, *Trade Up: How to Move From Just Making Money to Making a Difference* (Grand Rapids: Baker Books, 2017), 53.

[31] Lorin Woolfe, *Leadership Secrets From the Bible* (New York: MJF Books, 2002), 213.

The choice that Jesus made to share leadership was a catalyst for the transformation of the world.

> "The fruit of your labor grows on other people's trees."

If you do not feel accountable for identifying and developing leaders, a Seamless Pastoral Transition in which you overlap in service with an incoming pastor is probably not a good idea. If you haven't been in the habit of sharing leadership, it is unlikely that you will be able to share leadership with your successor when it matters most. One pastor told me that he couldn't imagine sharing the pulpit, even with an incoming pastor, because he was determined to preach every sermon he possibly could for the rest of his life. If that describes you, I recommend that you just retire when you want to (or have to) and let the church default to the Interim Model.

But if you are a pastor who thinks that Seamless Pastoral Transition is in the best interests of your church, sharing leadership must be a strong consideration. When the outgoing pastor shares leadership with the incoming pastor, it builds the credibility of the incoming pastor with the congregation. It also demonstrates to the incoming pastor the positive impact of shared leadership. And while it is wise for any pastor to develop leaders, it is critical for a pastor who is considering leading a Seamless Pastoral Transition. An outgoing

> An outgoing pastor's successor *may* come from outside of the church, but if they don't develop leaders, their successor *must* come from outside of the church.

32

pastor's successor *may* come from outside of the church, but if they don't develop leaders, their successor *must* come from outside of the church.

For your consideration: Would the people in your congregation who know you best consider you to be a leader who is deeply committed to developing other leaders and sharing leadership?

CHAPTER THREE

The Second Imperative:
Pave the Way

A s an NFL head coach, Tony Dungy led his teams to the playoffs for ten consecutive years. He coached the Indianapolis Colts to a Super Bowl victory in 2007, the first such win by an African American head coach. In addition to emerging as a respected analyst on NBC's *Football Night in America*, he is a prolific author and is in high demand as a speaker. But Tony Dungy has had a higher priority than personal accomplishments. He lives his life to pave the way for others.

Tony Dungy is clear concerning what his life is all about. "Winning the Super Bowl is not the ultimate victory. It's about the journey— mine and yours—and the lives we can touch, the legacy

> "Winning the Super Bowl is not the ultimate victory. It's about the journey—mine and yours—and the lives we can touch, the legacy we can leave, and the world we can change for the better."

we can leave, and the world we can change for the better."[32] He believes that a leader's commitment to pave the way for other leaders creates organizations that can "live on through succeeding generations. It means building with a

---

[32] Tony Dungy, *Quiet Strength: The Principles, Practices & Priorities of a Winning Life* (Carol Stream, IL: Tyndale, 2007), xv.

long-term perspective—a perspective that says when God is involved in the process, life takes on eternal significance."[33]

In a recent interview, I heard Tony Dungy share a story about Mike Tomlin, who had served under Dungy as an Assistant Coach. Mike Tomlin coached and mentored a football player named Scott Frost. Scott Frost, with Mike Tomlin's encouragement, became a college football coach. When Scott Frost arrived at the Dungy household to recruit Tony Dungy's son, Tony noted, "It was Scott Frost speaking to my son, but I heard Mike Tomlin's voice!" Tony Dungy influenced Mike Tomlin. Mike Tomlin influenced Scott Frost. Scott Frost ended up influencing Tony Dungy's son. It is a great example of the impact of investing in others.

In his book, *Uncommon: Finding Your Path to Significance*, Tony writes, "God knew before you were born that you would be where you are today. He knew that you would have influence over those whom you do, and He already knows those you will impact down the line. Through it all, the legacy you leave—the imprint that your life leaves on this earth—will determine what your life on earth meant."[34] Tony Dungy lives his life to pave the way for the success of others. As a result, his influence will be felt for generations to come.

---

[33] Tony Dungy, *The Mentor Leader: Secrets to Building People and Teams That Win Consistently* (Tyndale House Publishers, Carol Stream, IL, 2010),15.

[34] Tony Dungy, *Uncommon: Finding Your Path to Significance* (Carol Stream, IL: Tyndale, 2011), 216.

Recent research by Development Dimensions International (DDI) found that developing the next generation of leaders was at the top of the list of things that keep CEOs up at night. The DDI research study involved 15,000 leaders from 1,700 organizations in twenty-four major industry sectors. It states, "Developing new leaders and finding and upskilling current leaders with the potential to grow is crucial to future success. Companies must adopt a new model for leadership, driven by the idea that 'everyone is a leader' and that leadership must be developed continuously."[35] It's no wonder that a high percentage of corporate leaders have a commitment similar to that of Tony Dungy—a commitment to develop and pave the way for emerging leaders in their organizations.

Unfortunately, it is easier to observe passion for paving the way for next generation leaders in the sports world and corporate world than it is in the church world. Todd Adkins points out, "We play in an infinite game, and eternity hangs in the balance of what we do. Yet the local high school football coach likely focuses more time, energy, and development on his team's bench strength than the church down the street focuses on its leadership pipeline and bench strength. This should not

> Unfortunately, it is easier to observe passion for paving the way for next generation leaders in the sports world and corporate world than it is in the church world.

---

[35] Stephanie Neal, Jazmine Boatman and Bruce Watt, *Global Leadership Forecast* (Pittsburgh, PA: Development Dimensions International, 2021)

be the case."[36] Adkins notes that effective leadership succession, which is critical in the church, requires both a plan and a pipeline of emerging leaders. Conscientious church leaders must take on the responsibility of paving the way for the future leaders of the church.

Elijah and David Both Paved the Way

The prophet Elijah was one of kind. It was Elijah, along with Moses, who appeared with Jesus on the Mount of Transfiguration (Matthew 17). Elijah had an intimate relationship with God, and he was used by God to perform remarkable miracles. Elijah spoke to the people of Israel on behalf of God, even when the message was not easy to hear. With God's guidance, Elijah chose his successor: "So he set out from there, and found Elisha son of Shaphat, who was plowing. There were twelve yoke of oxen ahead of him, and he was with the twelfth. Elijah passed by him and threw his mantle over him." (1 Kings 19:19)

Elisha accepted Elijah's invitation. It was likely that Elisha had heard about Elijah's courage in confronting the corruption of Ahab and Jezebel and the miracle on Mount Carmel. As Elisha shadowed Elijah, he witnessed firsthand how Elijah provided leadership for the prophetic community of Israel and how Elijah provided spiritual leadership for the nation of Israel during the reigns of multiple kings. Elijah served as both master and mentor to Elisha, whose respect for Elijah was clearly seen when Elijah's life

---

[36] Todd Adkins, *Pipeline: Succession at Every Level* (Nashville: LifeWay Christian Resources, 2017), 22.

neared its end. Elisha would not let Elijah out of his sight and, before Elijah was miraculously escorted into heaven, Elisha submitted his famous request, "Please let me inherit a double share of your spirit." (2 Kings 2:9)

Elisha could not replace Elijah. No one could. But Elijah boldly stepped into the role that Elijah had held. Like Elijah, Elisha provided leadership for the prophetic community of Israel and he provided spiritual leadership for the nation of Israel during the reigns of multiple kings. And, as God had performed miracles through Elijah, God performed miracles through Elisha. It was well known that Elijah had chosen to mentor Elisha, so it is no surprise that those who honored and respected the leadership of Elijah also honored and respected the leadership of Elisha. One key to the successful ministry of Elisha was that Elijah intentionally paved the way.

As Elijah paved the way for Elisha, David paved the way for Solomon. When David neared the end of his life, he was made aware that his son, Adonijah, proclaimed himself to be David's successor. Even though Adonijah had the support of some significant leaders of Israel, David made it clear that he was the one who would choose his successor. David had Zadok the priest and Nathan the prophet anoint Solomon as his successor. He told them, "Blow the trumpet, and say, 'Long live King Solomon!' You shall go up following him. Let him enter and sit on my throne; he shall be king in my place, for I have appointed him to be ruler over Israel and over Judah." (1 Kings 1:34-35) Despite the fact that David had several sons and that there were other effective leaders in Israel, David made it clear that Solomon was his choice as successor. Given Solomon's profound wisdom, it is safe to assume that David had mentored Solomon with this succession in mind.

But it was more than just a public declaration that demonstrates how David paved the way for Solomon. David would have loved to have overseen the construction of the Temple. However, he knew that the construction would be left to his successor. He also knew that Solomon was "young and inexperienced" (1 Chronicles 29:1). So instead of leaving it up to Solomon to start from scratch, David put everything into place in order to set up Solomon for success. He gave him architectural plans for the entire temple and lined up the workers who would build it. "David said further to his son Solomon, 'Be strong and of good courage, and act. Do not be afraid or dismayed, for the Lord God, my God, is with you. He will not fail you or forsake you, until all the work for the service of the house of the Lord is finished. Here are the divisions of the priests and the Levites for all the service of the house of God, and with you in all the work will be every volunteer who has skill for any kind of service; also the officers and all the people will be wholly at your command.'" (1 Chronicles 28:20-21) In providing the plans and the materials and lining up the craftsmen for the construction of the Temple, David demonstrated his commitment to pave the way for Solomon.

As with Elijah and Elisha, the story of David and Solomon is a story of seamless leadership transition. Just as Elijah prepared the way for Elisha, David prepared the way for Solomon. Bradley Franc compares leadership succession to a well-planned relay race. He writes, "One of the most vital parts of a relay race is the handoff of the baton. Some of the greatest runners in the world have lost because of a bad handoff during a relay race. As the business owner in charge of your business, you are holding the baton. It is your job to run your portion of the race as best you can. To be successful in this role, however, you can't just think about running fast, or about the baton handoff, or how fast the guy in front of you is running. Instead, you must consider *all three*."[37] Conscientious leaders are diligent, not haphazard, in their approach to leadership transition. As Elijah paved the way for Elisha and David paved the way for Solomon, a conscientious leader will pave the way for their successor to ensure a truly effective handoff.

> As Elijah paved the way for Elisha and David paved the way for Solomon, a conscientious leader will pave the way for their successor to ensure a truly effective handoff.

Paving the Way at Macedonia Church

Macedonia Baptist Church was founded in the early 1900s. Situated in the Northeast region of the United States, the church is affiliated with a historic Black denomination. Over the decades, Macedonia Church became the place of worship and a thriving community of faith for many blacks who

---

[37] Bradley J. Franc, *The Succession Solution: The Strategic Guide to Business Transition* (Coppell, TX: Woodview Publishing Company, 2019), 10.

had migrated from the south seeking better job opportunities in the north.

Macedonia Church, of course, experienced many pastoral transitions over the decades. As with many congregational churches, when a pastor left his role, a search committee made up of church members worked together to identify one or more appropriate candidates for role of Senior Pastor. A congregational vote confirmed who the next pastor would be. The time frame between permanent pastors varied from months to years.

The outgoing pastor of Macedonia Church took the office of Senior Pastor in the late 1980s. He was a larger-than-life leader and, under his direction, the church experienced tremendous growth, growing to over 3,000 members. Dozens of ministries were established that impacted thousands of lives inside and outside of the church, including a ministry focused on economic development and housing in the community served by the church.

Black churches have unique challenges related to pastoral succession. Ralph Watkins writes, "The richness of the African American pastoral tradition has been rooted in the loyal connection of pastor to congregation. Once again, this is a product of our history. Our pastors have led every movement to come out of the African American community. These movements go back to our earliest times in America. It was our religious leaders who gave their all for our freedom from the evils of slavery. If we fast-forward to the twentieth century, we once again see it in the civil rights-era pastors who put their lives on the line for our freedom movements."[38]

Watkins builds on this observation by pointing out one challenge that Black churches face when it comes to pastoral transition. "Perhaps more than any mainline church culture, churches in the African American community are facing massive pastoral transition. . . . When it is time for a transition from one pastor to the next, we can only expect that old loyalties will remain, and rightly so, as a result of this unique bond we form with our pastors during their tenure as our leaders. The question becomes, how do we move on—honoring old loyalties while building new ones?"[39] According to the Barna Group's 2021 study on trends in the Black Church, "The pastor within the Black Church has historically served as spiritual leader, social advocate, cultural curator, first responder and wise sage. Churchgoers and non-churchgoers alike tell Barna how incredibly important this figure is in their lives and communities."[40] While this does not minimize the importance of the pastor in non-Black churches, it definitely is

> "Perhaps more than any mainline church culture, churches in the African American community are facing massive pastoral transition."

---

[38] Ralph C. Watkins, *Leading Your African American Church Through Pastoral Transition* (Valley Forge, PA: Judson Press, 2010), 34.

[39] Ralph C. Watkins, *Leading Your African American Church Through Pastoral Transition*, 2.

[40] Barna Group. *Trends in the Black Church: Celebrating its Legacy and Investing in a Hopeful Future.* (Ventura, CA: Barna Group, 2021), Page 99.

a factor that cannot be ignored when considering pastoral succession in the Black Church.

The Barna study notes, "When it comes to pastoral succession and transitions of leadership, most Black Church pastors feel reluctant to give up the pulpit. Many believe this should only take place if a pastor is unable to perform their duties due to age, illness or death."[41] Accordingly, less than half of Black Church leaders over the age of sixty plan to retire in the next ten years, and only thirteen percent of Black Church pastors say their church is well prepared for a leadership transition.[42]

After leading Macedonia Church for over two decades, the outgoing pastor knew how important he was in the lives of his parishioners and in the community. He also knew that his tenure as pastor was coming to an end—especially since he was dealing with various health challenges. The outgoing pastor was deeply passionate about the church maintaining its city-changing momentum and he made the decision to pave the way for his successor.

For five years, the outgoing pastor observed first-hand the leadership capabilities of one of his Associate Pastors, who he became convinced was the right person to become the incoming pastor of Macedonia Church. He felt strongly that a Seamless Pastoral Transition was best for the church and that a search committee was not needed. He advocated that the board of directors amend the church by-laws to allow an Associate Pastor to assume the role of Senior

---

[41] Barna Group, *Trends in the Black Church*, 141.

[42] Barna Group, *Trends in the Black Church*, 137.

Pastor. Before the congregational vote took place, he publicly endorsed the Associate Pastor as the next Senior Pastor. The beloved outgoing pastor died four years later, but not before seeing the incoming pastor spark a new season of growth and vitality for Macedonia Church.

The incoming pastor, unsurprisingly, is an advocate for Seamless Pastoral Transitions. He said, "I know how vulnerable Black Churches are to trauma and even church splits during pastoral transitions. Senior Pastors in Black Churches have extraordinary respect and influence. Their congregations often see the Senior Pastor as irreplaceable, which is why so many Senior Pastors of Black Churches die in office."

> "Senior Pastors in Black Churches have extraordinary respect and influence. Their congregations often see the Senior Pastor as irreplaceable, which is why so many Senior Pastors of Black Churches die in office."

Macedonia Church maintained its positive momentum, due in large part because the outgoing pastor, out of his deep commitment to the ongoing health and well-being of the church, paved the way for the incoming pastor.

Paving the Way at St. John's Church

As with the outgoing pastor at Macedonia Church, the Senior Pastor of St. John's Church of Highland felt that his church would be best served by a Seamless Pastoral Transition. As the time for his retirement drew near, he became convinced that the Associate Pastor who was serving St. John's Church at the time was the right person to take on the Senior Pastor role at St. John's. After all, his Associate Pastor had faithfully served the 250 members of St. John's Church of Highland for thirteen years. She both understood and embraced the mission of the church and she was loved and respected by the congregation. She also understood and appreciated the unique culture of St. John's that somehow made everyone feel welcome despite their differences—including differences in political persuasions. St. John's Church of Highland could genuinely be described as a family.

However, there was a problem. St. John's is a part of the Evangelical Lutheran Church in America (ELCA), a mainline denomination with clear restrictions on the involvement of an outgoing pastor in the selection of the incoming pastor. In addition, congregational policy connected the Associate Pastor's call to the Senior Pastor's call, creating a complex process if the Associate Pastor would want to stay. It would have been much easier for the outgoing pastor of St. John's to just retire and let the standard process play out. Instead, he met with his Bishop to discuss the possibility of a Seamless Pastoral Transition.

The Bishop overseeing St. John's Church approached the situation with an open mind. He reflected on the typical process, which includes the Bishop appointing an interim pastor,

> According to the Bishop, "This uniform process worked well for many years, especially when there were several viable candidates for each open position. However, the edges of the system are fraying and exceptions to the rule must be considered."

who signs renewable contracts, and the establishment of a Call Committee, all culminating in a congregational vote on one final candidate after considering one or more external candidates. According to the Bishop, "This uniform process worked well for many years, especially when there were several viable candidates for each open position. However, the edges of the system are fraying and exceptions to the rule must be considered."

Heifetz and Linsky write, "We have to learn new ways because without learning new ways – changing attitudes, values, and behaviors – people cannot make the adaptive leap necessary to thrive in the new environment."[43] Such forward-thinking applies to all organizations, including churches. Knowing that the average time between permanent pastors in the current system was two to three years and being well aware of the positive momentum of St. John's Church, the Bishop supported the outgoing pastor's proposal of a Seamless Pastoral Transition.

> "We have to learn new ways because without learning new ways – changing attitudes, values, and behaviors – people cannot make the adaptive leap necessary to thrive in the new environment."

The approach of the outgoing pastor was pivotal. During the course of their years of joint ministry, he often stated, "We are the pastors of St. John's Church" rather

---

[43] Ronald A. Heifetz and Marty Linsky, *Leadership on the Line: Staying Alive Through the Dangers of Leadership* (Boston: Harvard Business School Press, 2002), 13.

than "I am the pastor of St. John's Church." During the final year of his tenure, he publicly recognized the significant contributions of the Associate Pastor. His public affirmation was coupled with a high level of empowerment and shared leadership. The Associate Pastor shared many ministry roles with the Senior Pastor, which included delivering the sermon in approximately fifty percent of the weekend services at St. John's.

It is interesting to note that the Associate Pastor at St. John's Church of Highland, due to congregational requirements, had to submit her resignation when the Senior Pastor left. She had to wait thirty days before the congregational vote could take place that confirmed her as the new Senior Pastor. Despite the unsettledness she felt during those thirty days, she reflected positively on the transition: "I had what amounted to a thirteen-year interview process. As Associate Pastor, I built a lot of trusted relationships. We did a lot of good work together and, once I was called as Senior Pastor, I was able to just pick up on the momentum that already existed and build on it." The Seamless Pastoral Transition at St. John's Church was a resounding success. There is no doubt that a key reason why was because the Bishop and the outgoing pastor helped to pave the way.

> The Seamless Pastoral Transition at St. John's Church was a resounding success. There is no doubt that a key reason why was because the Bishop and the outgoing pastor helped to pave the way.

Paving the Way at Amplify Church

The process outlined in the church bylaws for replacing the Senior Pastor of Amplify Church involved the establishment of a search committee made up of church members who would identify potential candidates. Candidates would then be interviewed and speak at the church until one candidate received a majority of votes from the congregation. This process occurred three times in our church history. Each time it resulted in major destabilization in the church. In every transition, a significant percentage of the people who voted "no" for the incoming Senior Pastor left the church.

To reduce the length and the trauma of the pastoral transition process, the Amplify Church board of directors revised the church bylaws to make it the responsibility of the Senior Pastor to nominate a successor to the board. Assuming the person nominated is approved, it becomes the responsibility of the Senior Pastor to mentor that person to be ready to step in when needed. Whether the Senior Pastor is suddenly gone for unexpected reasons or a transition is several years away, the successor has been identified and an immediate transition can take place.

Within five years of returning to the Senior Pastor role at Amplify Church, I proposed an "emergency successor" to the church Board of Directors. Although I was in my early fifties and in good health, I knew that anything could happen that could lead to my sudden departure. In the years that followed, I spent a significant amount of time developing a personal relationship with my emergency successor, who ended up years later becoming my actual successor as Senior Pastor of Amplify. I gave him many opportunities to grow as a leader through both formal and informal learning experiences. I provided him with timely and specific positive feedback and feedback for improvement. Most of all, I gave him many opportunities to prove his effectiveness as a leader, including leading a new extension campus.

Two years before the handoff of the Senior Pastor role at Amplify, I worked with two external coaches and our church board to develop a formal pastoral transition plan. During those two years, the incoming pastor's responsibilities were elevated. He went from speaking during weekend services once every couple of months to once a month. During my final year as Senior Pastor, the incoming pastor spoke half of the time. During my final few months as Senior Pastor, he regularly led staff meetings and board meetings while I was present. I poured into my successor what I knew about church leadership to pave the way for his success.

Marshall Goldsmith gives advice to business leaders about their leadership transition, "Involve your successor in all important decisions and, to the degree humanly possible, make sure that she agrees with your long-term strategies—before they are announced. Remember, she is the person who is going to

> "Don't worry about 'finishing on a great note.' Be more focused on putting your successor in a position where *she* will succeed than finishing in a way that will make you look good."

have to live with these strategies for the next few years— and make them work. Make those tough, unpopular decisions that you know are good for the company. Don't worry about 'finishing on a great note.' Be more focused on putting your successor in a position where *she* will succeed than finishing in a way that will make you look good."[44]

One of my commitments in paving the way for my successor related to changes that he wanted to make at Amplify Church. We prayerfully discussed those changes in detail. Then I led the way in making many of the changes that were in my successor's heart *before* the transition. That way, the changes were made leveraging the trust and credibility I had with the congregation. These changes included:

> I led the way in making many of the changes that were in my successor's heart *before* the transition. That way, the changes were made leveraging the trust and credibility I had with the congregation.

+ **Multi-site strategy** – I was comfortable with having one campus with multiple services until extension campuses were absolutely necessary. My successor felt that our church's vision, "to lead as many people as possible into a growing relationship with Jesus Christ," would be better served by a multi-site approach. Given his passion and willingness to provide leadership for new campuses, I introduced the multi-site model to the church

---

[44] Marshall Goldsmith, *Succession: Are You Ready?* (Boston: Harvard Business Press, 2009), 12.

with my full endorsement. When one of the new campuses did not work out, I led the process of spinning it off into an independent church three months before leaving my role as Senior Pastor.

+ **Church Name Change** – Years before the transition, I felt that we needed to change the name of the church, which at the time was Pittsburgh East Community Church. The name worked well when we only served the eastern suburbs of Pittsburgh. Once we added more campuses, we needed a name that was not tied to a single location. While there were many options, the fact that my successor's preference was Amplify Church settled the debate.

+ **Church Staff and Board Members** – In the final two to three years of my tenure, I made no staff changes or changes to the church Board of Directors without my successor's involvement. He would soon be the one who would lead the people whose names were on our organizational chart. While there were inevitable staff member and board member changes that took place after the transition, I led the way on way on making several changes *before* the transition that reduced the number of staff and board challenges that my successor would need to address.

- **Facility Changes** – We changed the primary paint color of the sanctuary of our main campus from white to dark gray to make it feel more intimate. We invested in new audio, video and lighting equipment at prices that, at least at first, gave me sticker shock. We added new signage inside and outside of our church campuses, including some vintage neon signage. Although I actually ended up liking the changes to our facilities, they sure as heck were not my idea. I led the changes because they were important to my successor.

I never felt that any of the decisions I made that were based on my successor's preferences were inconsistent with our church mission, beliefs, or values. They were just about preferences. He would have to live with the changes a lot longer than I. It was about to be his turn to lead, so I paved the way.

Paving the Way—a Christ-Centered Reflection

Jesus paved the way for His disciples to effectively take His message to the world. He taught them, mentored them and prayed for them. He sent the Holy Spirit to empower them. Lorin Wolfe writes, "Perhaps the biggest test for leaders is their ability to 'let go,' surrendering the reins of power to well-prepared successors. Mature leaders realize when the time is near for them to leave the stage, and they anticipate this by gradually transferring the trappings and reality of power to their proteges. And lest you feel that it would be impossible to find a more capable pair of hands than your own, consider the words of Jesus Christ, who many believe to be the very embodiment of perfection. He expressed supreme confidence in his followers' ability not just to 'do what I have been doing' but to 'do even greater things than these.'"[45]

> "Mature leaders realize when the time is near for them to leave the stage, and they anticipate this by gradually transferring the trappings and reality of power to their proteges."

Jesus paved the way for his disciples in a manner that should inspire us to pave the way for the next generation of leaders, whether or not those leaders are in a formal succession plan. Paving the way for next generation leaders must be a priority for church leaders. While leaders cannot guarantee what will happen to their organizations under new leadership, they must do more than just hope and pray that things work out. By paving the way, outgoing pastors can increase the chances that their successors and their churches can enter a new season of effective ministry.

The apostle Paul wrote about something that all Christians should aspire to, "Do nothing from selfish ambition or empty conceit, but in humility regard others as better than yourselves. Let each of you look not to your own interests, but to the interests of others. Let the same mind be in you that was in Christ Jesus." (Philippians 2:3-5) Pastors, denominational executives, and church

---

[45] Lorin Woolfe, *Leadership Secrets From the Bible* (New York: MJF Books, 2002), 216.

board members all need to allow these words to inspire their actions, including a willingness to sacrifice personal preferences. In doing so, you are serving as a living example of one who knows that your church ultimately belongs to Jesus Christ.

> *For your consideration: What are the practical things that you are doing to pave the way for the person who will lead your church when your tenure ends?*

CHAPTER FOUR

The Third Imperative: Model Humility

Humility doesn't come naturally to leaders, but it can be observed in the lives of the best leaders. For over forty years, *Leadership Foundations* has brought leaders together for the good of their cities, with a particular focus on positively influencing the lives of those who live in underserved communities. Leadership Foundations (LF) was founded in Pittsburgh in 1978 by Reid Carpenter, who was a leader at Young Life, a ministry that introduces middle school, high school, and college students to Jesus Christ and helps them to grow in their faith. Reid Carpenter was inspired to establish the Pittsburgh Leadership Foundation by the prayer of Sam Shoemaker voiced in the mid-1950s, "that Pittsburgh will one day be as famous for God as it is (today) for steel."[46]

During the 1980s, Leadership Foundations spread in cities across the United States including Philadelphia, Memphis, Denver, Phoenix, and Chicago, among leaders with a heart for the transformation of their cities. The programs implemented by Leadership Foundations, which varied from city to city, addressed issues that included

---

[46] Time Magazine, *Religion: God & Steel in Pittsburgh* (New York: Time, Inc., March 21, 1955)

youth mentoring, affordable housing, food insecurity and support for families of those who were incarcerated. Recognizing its significant impact, the U.S. Department of Human Services and the U.S. Department of Justice provided more than $18 million in grants to Leadership Foundations. In the 1990s, the Leadership Foundation's model of city transformation began to spread globally to cities in Africa, India, Central America and the Caribbean.

In 2006, Reid Carpenter, the President of Leadership Foundations, initiated a seamless leadership succession process with the LF board. He was sixty-eight years old. As Reid states, "Technology was outpacing me and I didn't feel that I was the right person to take Leadership Foundations into the future. Personally, it was time for me to hit the brake instead of the gas pedal." Fortunately, a number of proven leaders had evolved in the organization, many of whom were Presidents of Leadership Foundations in their cities. In 2008, Dave Hillis, President of the Northwest Leadership Foundation in Tacoma, Washington, was appointed the new President of Leadership Foundations.

Reid and Dave overlapped in their service of LF for several months, with Dave gaining valuable experience and insights while Reid was still in office, particularly related to navigating the financial realities of leading a global organization. Their seamless leadership transition was a resounding success, and the organization continued to grow in impact under Dave's leadership, including the establishment of the Colangelo Carpenter Innovation Center to generate and scale innovative programs, practices, and partnerships to support cities around the world.

There were many factors in the successful seamless transition at Leadership Foundations. Perhaps the most profound factor was that both Reid and Dave modeled humility in the way that they honored one another. Reid had a choice, as he puts it, to hang on to LF or to let go. He chose to let go. As founder and legendary leader, Reid had to intentionally get out of the way. He purposely moved into a supporting role, with the goal of serving Dave. "I didn't want to tie his hands, or to be the old guy looking over my successor's shoulder," Reid recalls. "As a result, I declined to sit on the LF Board of Directors. It had been my board. Now it had to become Dave's board."

Reid made the commitment to never second guess Dave's decisions from the sidelines. That wasn't easy. There were days when Reid felt relieved that he was not making the decisions about the direction of Leadership Foundations. There were other days, of course, that he felt like his decisions would be better than the decisions made by his successor. On those days, unless Dave asked, Reid swallowed his opinion. Reid's advice to outgoing leaders is simple, "You need to know why you left and where you are going. The more you know where you are going, the more free you will be in letting go. Your day to day affirmation needs to come from someplace else."

On the other hand, Dave intentionally honored Reid and the groundwork that Reid had laid. He did not fall into the trap that many incoming leaders fall into of acting like they have arrived on the scene to save the day. One thing was keenly felt by both Reid and Dave. Neither ever questioned one another's sincere support. They spoke every two to three weeks, particularly about threshold issues about which Dave solicited Reid's advice. It meant a lot to Dave that Reid could talk about issues and options without being pushy. As Dave puts it, "When Reid let go, he let go. I was so grateful."

As a Christ-centered leader, Dave Hillis admires the words of the apostle Paul, who wrote to his protégé Timothy, "I have finished the race." (2 Timothy 4:7) He doesn't believe that Paul was describing a marathon. He believes, given Paul's commitment to mentor Timothy as an emerging leader, that Paul was describing a relay race. Paul had not reached the finish line, it just was time for him to pass the baton. Dave notes, "I am merely a steward, and I must know that a time will come for me to hand things off to the next leader." In 2022, Dave handed off the baton by leading a seamless leadership transition with his successor.

I have a unique insight into Leadership Foundations. Eight months after I left my role as Senior Pastor of Amplify Church, I accepted the position of President of the Pittsburgh Leadership Foundation. It was a significant task to carry on the legacy of the organization that started the worldwide LF movement. I have had the opportunity of getting to know both Reid Carpenter and Dave Hillis. I have never heard a word of criticism from either about the other. They are very different from one another, and yet they seem to be one another's biggest cheerleaders. They both have made their ego needs secondary to the well-being of the organization. In that regard, they have been genuinely Christ-like in the way they have modeled humility.

"He must increase, but I must decrease"

One of the most powerful gospel passages focuses on the frame of mind that John the Baptist adopted when he realized that Jesus had arrived on the scene. John had made it clear, "One who is more powerful than I is coming; I am not worthy to untie the strap of his sandals" (Luke 3:16). Though John the Baptist clearly saw himself as paving the way for Jesus, it must have been hard to think about his successful, prominent ministry fading away. John was a proven leader with many followers. He had preached to and baptized hundreds, if not thousands of people. People came from far and wide to experience his ministry.

Human nature suggests that John the Baptist would have had thoughts like, "God has used me in so many ways. Certainly, God is not finished with me. Certainly, I am not meant to just hand over my followers to another." If John the Baptist had any such thoughts, he hid them well. When his followers questioned him about the situation, he declared, "He who has the bride is the bridegroom. The friend of the bridegroom who stands and hears him rejoices greatly at the bridegroom's voice. For this reason my joy has been fulfilled. He must increase, but I must decrease" (John 3:29-30). Even though he had a powerful and widely respected ministry, John the Baptist held that ministry loosely, knowing that his ministry was not about himself. He needed to humbly point people to Jesus.

Norman Cohen points out, "Every leader must let go at some point, ceding leadership to the next generation. Mature leaders realize when the time is near for them to leave the stage, though surrendering power is rarely easy. However, their handing over the mantle in a gracious and supportive manner is crucial for a sense of continuity."[47] Unfortunately, pride can get in the way in any organization, including churches. The Lead Pastor has a highly influential role—particularly in a thriving church. It is difficult to give up a position that results in daily expressions of love and respect from church and community members. This is especially true if the pastor is also the founding pastor, or if the pastor has had a significant role in shaping a unique mission and role in the community that the church is fulfilling.

Yet, the outgoing pastor who genuinely cares about the people and ministry of the church will do everything possible to humbly transfer their leadership to their successor. It is not an easy task. As Tom Mullins observes, "I think that one of the most difficult things for a lot of outgoing leaders is simply stepping away from everything they've built and invested in for a significant number of years. Often, it has become the platform for their credibility as leaders and value as individuals. A change in that role

[47] Norman J. Cohen, *Moses and the Journey to Leadership: Timeless Lessons of Effective Management from the Bible and Today's Leaders* (Woodstock, VT: Jewish Lights Publishing, 2007), 166.

threatens their security and identity. My greatest advice in preparing yourself is to plan thoughtfully and pray for humility."[48]

It is important to note that the outgoing pastor isn't the only one with the imperative of modeling humility. Instead of dismissing the ministry of John the Baptist as "old news," Jesus said, "Truly I tell you, among those born of women no one has arisen greater than John the Baptist" (Matt. 11:11). The honor that Jesus showed to John the Baptist should inspire every incoming pastor to humbly look for ways to honor the outgoing pastor.

> "My greatest advice in preparing yourself is to plan thoughtfully and pray for humility."

We know there was no jealousy or resentment in Jesus regarding John the Baptist. It would seem that there was no jealousy or resentment in John the Baptist regarding Jesus. Despite these inspiring examples, humility is perhaps the most elusive characteristic that Christian leaders are called to model. One thing is certain, when pastors with extraordinary leadership gifts overlap in their service to a congregation in a Seamless Pastoral Transition, sincere humility—or lack thereof—will be on full display for the congregation.

Perhaps John the Baptist's words are a perfect description

> Perhaps John the Baptist's words are a perfect description of how a humble outgoing pastor should think of the incoming pastor—"He must increase, but I must decrease."

---

[48] Tom Mullins, *Passing the Leadership Baton: A Winning Transition Plan for Your Ministry* (Nashville: Thomas Nelson, 2015), 38,46.

of how a humble outgoing pastor should think of the incoming pastor—"He must increase, but I must decrease." Andrew Flowers considers John's approach to be a sign of the highest level of leadership, "This kind of slow fade is at the heart of every 'Level 5' leader. The ability to allow someone else to have the reins requires humility."[49] John the Baptist declared that his joy was made complete with the prominence of Jesus' ministry eclipsing his ministry, setting an extraordinary example for outgoing pastors.

Humility Modeled at Riverside Community Church

Riverside Community Church is part of the Assemblies of God, a historic Pentecostal tradition that is described not as a denomination but as a "voluntary cooperative fellowship." Hence, there is no required process that Riverside Community Church must follow for pastoral transitions, nor is there a denominational executive that oversees pastoral transitions at Riverside. The church is independent and self-governing and has its own set of by-laws to govern leadership succession.

When the outgoing pastor of Riverside Church reached his early sixties, he prayerfully determined that a Seamless Pastoral Transition was in the best interests of the church. He was the Founding Pastor of the church, and under his thirty-two-year tenure as Lead Pastor, the church had grown into a vital congregation with an average attendance

---

[49] Andrew Flowers, *Leading Through Succession: Why Pastoral Leadership is the Key to a Healthy Transition* (Coppell, TX: Independently Published, 2017), 114.

of approximately 750 people. In partnership with the church board of directors, the outgoing pastor chose an Associate Pastor of Riverside to become his successor.

The incoming pastor had faithfully served the church for more than eighteen years in various roles when he was approached about taking on the role of Lead Pastor. Through his time as Associate Pastor, the incoming pastor had been given the opportunity to develop as a leader and demonstrate his leadership effectiveness, including providing pastoral leadership for a second location/campus of Riverside Community Church. He had stepped up to the challenge and was sincerely admired by church members.

The outgoing and incoming pastors worked together to create a two-year plan that would culminate with a formal transition. During that two-year time, the incoming pastor was given the title of "Co-Lead Pastor" to signal to the congregation that his role had changed and that he was about to take on the formal Lead Pastor role. During the final year, he preached at approximately half of the weekend services at Riverside. With the incoming pastor having received an overwhelmingly positive congregational vote to take on the role of Lead Pastor, the Seamless Pastoral Transition at Riverside Community Church took place with no loss of momentum in the church.

One of the keys to the successful Seamless Pastoral Transition at Riverside was that both the outgoing pastor and incoming pastor modeled humility. They both committed early on to demonstrate mutual honor and to approach the transition with deference to one another.

They met regularly and had open discussions about their working relationship and the importance of a smooth succession. When either pastor felt that his toes were stepped on, they talked it through.

Modeling humility was not easy. As the founding pastor who had served the church for more than thirty years, the outgoing pastor deeply appreciated the regular expressions of love he received from the congregation. While he was happy to choose a successor and acknowledge that a transition would someday occur, it was much more difficult to commit to a specific handoff date that would be announced to the congregation. After all, he was relatively young in his early sixties and he had a lot left to give.

On the other hand, the incoming pastor felt that it was his time. He had served for eighteen years as an Associate Pastor and felt more than ready to take on the Lead Pastor Role. The incoming pastor felt it was important to agree on and communicate a formal transition date. It is no surprise that the two-year transition plan they agreed to felt too short for the outgoing pastor and too long for the incoming pastor! Even with a formal transition plan, it would not be easy for the outgoing pastor to let go. Nor would it be easy for the incoming pastor to be patient.

How did they demonstrate their commitment to model humility? Both pastors referred to experiences from the life of King David. The outgoing pastor said about the incoming pastor, "He never had an 'Absalom spirit' and he never undermined me, even when we had disagreements." The incoming pastor said about the outgoing pastor, "He never had a 'Saul spirit' and never threw spears at me—literally or figuratively!" The hard work that they put into their relationship was evident to the church. In a world where leaders are seldom accused of being humble, the outgoing and incoming pastors of Riverside Community Church were living examples of humility to the people of their church.

> The outgoing pastor said about the incoming pastor, "He never had an 'Absalom spirit' and he never undermined me, even when we had disagreements." The incoming pastor said about the outgoing pastor, "He never had a 'Saul spirit' and never threw spears at me—literally or figuratively!"

It is important to note that both pastors are convinced that showing humility and honor *after* the transition was equally as important as showing humility and honor *before* the transition. The incoming pastor was and is careful to not to adopt the commonly held "out with the old and in with the new" attitude. While he has a fresh vision for Riverside Community Church, he doesn't speak in terms of a brand new vision but instead speaks in terms of building on the foundation that had been laid. The outgoing pastor, who is still actively involved as a member of Riverside, does not enter into conversations with church members about comparing his style of leadership to the leadership style of his successor. The united front that they worked so hard to build before the transition is still intact after the transition. They seem to know the truth behind the words of Jerry David and Steve Sells, who write, "Success rates spike once a paradigm of mutual honor is established between the predecessor and successor."[50] Mutual honor and modeling humility are seen by both the outgoing and incoming pastors as critical to the ongoing health of Riverside Community Church.

> "Success rates spike once a paradigm of mutual honor is established between the predecessor and successor."

Humility Modeled at St. Stephen's Anglican Church

Unlike Riverside Community Church, St. Stephen's Anglican Church did not have an option to adopt a Seamless Pastoral Transition. St. Stephen's is a part of the Anglican Church in North America, a mainline denomination that embraces the Interim Model. Once the pastor (rector) leaves, the church is considered "vacant" until a new rector is installed, typically for a one-to-two-year period.

Having served as rector for twenty-four years, the sixty-nine-year old outgoing pastor of St. Stephen's Anglican Church was on a bike ride when he felt like God whispered the words to him, "It's time." He gave a one year notice, but was determined that St. Stephen's would not experience a traumatic pastoral transition. He knew from experience that during the vacancies between rectors, even when an interim rector is involved, the churches in his denomination commonly dipped in attendance, giving, vision, momentum, and mission. Ministries of the church such as

---

[50] Jerry W. David and Steve Sells, *Honorable Design: The Art and the Order of Generational Transition* (Evington, VA: Brookstone Publishing Group, 2019), 7.

community service suffered. His hope was to work with the church search committee to identify a successor and plan for a seamless transition.

Perhaps this is a good time to discuss the common practice of using a search committee to identify a church's incoming pastor. A search committee is typically composed of members of the church who are charged with identifying potential candidates to become the next pastor. The search committee then determines one or more "finalists" who are introduced to the congregation. A congregational vote typically determines who the next pastor will be.

Unfortunately, and understandably, search committee members typically lack the expertise that effective pastoral transition demands. Robert Dingman points out that a pastoral search committee should include a person with management know-how, someone who is theologically astute, a person with interviewing and assessment skills, a writer, someone with a feel for financial matters, someone with good logical and analytical abilities, perhaps a lawyer, a number of deeply spiritual people, and someone who knows the background of the organization and any denominational ties it may have.[51] He also lists the qualities that search committee members will ideally possess: they are eager to serve, not coerced into it. They have the available time. They are strong enough to speak up but not have dominating personalities. They have positive, can-do

---

[51] Robert W. Dingman, *In Search of a Leader: The Complete Search Committee Guidebook* (Westlake Village, CA: Lakeside Books, 1994), 23-25.

attitudes and good energy levels. They are fairly intelligent people. They have previously been effective committee members. They can maintain confidences (even from their spouses), and they are decisive people.[52] Dingman's list reflects the seriousness of the pastoral search process, but how many churches can put a committee of people together with these qualifications?

No matter how qualified, there is something critical that members of a search committee cannot comprehend— *the competencies the incoming pastor needs to effectively lead the church in a rapidly changing world.*

> No matter how qualified, there is something critical that members of a search committee cannot comprehend—*the competencies the incoming pastor needs to effectively lead the church in a rapidly changing world.*

As Michael J. Anthony and Mick Boersma remind us, Search committee members "are laypeople – few search committee members truly understand the unique nature and challenges of being in a pastoral position."[53] I personally have never met a layperson who truly understands the role and calling of a pastor. Only another pastor really gets it. One of my closest friends is the owner of a nationally recognized bakery. I know his business well—the facility, the equipment, the employees, and, of course, the products. I am often in his bakery several times a week. But despite my intimate knowledge of his business, it would be absurd

---

[52] Dingman, *In Search of a Leader*, 25-27.

[53] Michael J. Anthony and Mick Boersma, *Moving on Moving Forward: A Guide For Pastors in Transition* (Grand Rapids: Zondervan, 2007), 214.

for me to think that I should lead the process of choosing his successor while cutting him out of the process. I am not a baker. I have never owned or run a bakery.

With the full support of his Bishop, the outgoing pastor of St. Stephen's Anglican Church served as a consultant to the church search committee, which identified the next rector of St. Stephen's. This was extraordinary in and of itself. Another bishop in a similar denomination adamantly maintained that there must be a firewall between the outgoing pastor and the process for selecting an incoming pastor. He would put any outgoing pastor "under discipline" for even asking a church board member or search committee member about how the search process is going. The same bishop forbids outgoing pastors from being in contact with church members after they leave their role. Such policies seem to assume that no outgoing pastor could ever act with the best interests of the church and successor in mind. This is a false assumption.

In every case study covered in this paper that included a search committee (about half), the outgoing pastor was engaged with the search committee as a member or as an advisor/coach. In each case, the active involvement of the outgoing pastor leveraged that pastor's love for and knowledge of the congregation. It was wise for St. Stephen's Anglican Church to engage the help of their outgoing pastor in the search process. He had insights that no one else had or could have had. The search committee benefitted from their trusted outgoing pastor's valuable wisdom and experience.

As it turns out, although an internal candidate who had served on St. Stephen's staff was interviewed, an external candidate was hired as the incoming rector of St. Stephen's Anglican Church. A seven-week overlap was planned during which the outgoing rector and incoming rector would serve St. Stephen's together. Given the short overlap, they both knew that modeling humility and showing mutual honor was particularly critical for success.

A press release from the time of the transition quoted the outgoing rector as saying about the incoming rector and his spouse, "Their love for Christ, their breadth of experience and their passion for the mission of the gospel will be a great blessing to this church and the community." These were more than just words. The outgoing pastor genuinely let go, knowing it was time to conclude his years as rector. While still worshipping at St. Stephens with his family, the outgoing rector practiced the spiritual discipline of "relinquishment" and, as he puts it, he donned his Harry Potter "invisibility cloak!"

One of the first things that the incoming rector did was coordinate a celebration dinner to honor the outgoing rector and his many contributions to St. Stephen's. He arranged for the church to pay the travel expenses for the children of the outgoing rector to travel from around the country to be there. At the end of the celebration dinner, the outgoing rector and his spouse prayed for God's blessing on the incoming rector and his family. In turn, the incoming rector and his spouse prayed for God's blessing on the outgoing rector and his family. Then the Bishop prayed for

God's blessing on both families and for the entire congregation. A successful Seamless Pastoral Transition took place at St. Stephen's Anglican Church, thanks in large part to the outgoing rector and incoming rector honoring one another – and modeling humility.

> A successful Seamless Pastoral Transition took place at St. Stephen's Anglican Church, thanks in large part to the outgoing rector and incoming rector honoring one another – and modeling humility.

Modeling Humility at Amplify Church

As I consider the three Leadership Transition Imperatives, I believe that I was relatively effective as the outgoing pastor at sharing leadership. I was also relatively effective at paving the way for my successor. Not so much with modeling humility. I underestimated the emotions that I would experience. As I entered my sixties, I did not want to admit that I was not as passionate as I once was. I did not want to admit that I was not as open to change as I once was. I did not want to admit that I was not as dynamic in the pulpit. I did not want to admit that I was not as goal-oriented or creative as I once was. It was easy to avoid seeing these realities because I was surrounded by staff members and church members who loved and respected me and complimented me the same way they did when I was at the top of my game.

When I was sixty-three, we hired an external consultant to help us to create a detailed plan for the Seamless Pastoral Transition at Amplify Church. Even though I was planning that the formal transition would take place just before my sixty-seventh birthday, I knew that it was not too soon to put a specific plan together. After attending multiple church services, interviewing staff members and board members, and reviewing the results of a congregational survey, the consultant shared his findings. He felt confident that the incoming pastor had the gifts needed to lead Amplify Church. He felt that the church staff and board would support the incoming pastor and that the congregation was in a good place to handle change. In fact, the key words that emerged from the congregational survey taken after my successor had been announced indicated that Amplify Church members felt hopeful, thankful, excited, optimistic, and expectant. The consultant's report, which was completed three years before the original anticipated date for my transition, included these words, "All things considered, not only should you anticipate a smooth pastoral transition, but the timetable for that transition could be accelerated without concern."

I read those words and felt great that I had effectively shared leadership and prepared the way. I also felt confident that my successor would read the words about possibly accelerating the handoff and respond, "Lee, it is great that the consultant feels that I am ready, but I think we should stick to your original timeline." That was not his response. Instead, he made it clear that he was ready, and that the consultant's report confirmed that I was pushing the transition time too far into the future. I was shocked by the intensity of my feelings of defensiveness and anger.

My feelings were on full display at what my successor and I now affectionately call "The Dinner." Shortly after my successor expressed his feelings that the timetable should be accelerated, I invited him and his wife to join me and my wife at a nice local restaurant to hash things out over dinner. It wasn't long before I started asking some questions that turned the dinner from the kind of pleasant dinner we had shared as couples dozens of times into an evening of high tension.

> I was shocked by the intensity of my feelings of defensiveness and anger. My feelings were on full display at what my successor and I now affectionately call "The Dinner."

Since my successor had not expressed specifically why he was interested in accelerating the process, I provided the reasons for him. "If you have your eyes on a Senior Pastor's salary and don't want to wait, let's talk about how much more money you need to make now and I am sure I can work with the board to see what can be done." He insisted that his interest in accelerating the process was not about money, since he already was paid a generous salary. I then offered another option, "If it is not about money, it must be about power. If you want more power and authority in church leadership and decision making, I am sure I can work with the board to see what can be done." He insisted that his interest in accelerating the process was not about getting more power or authority, since he already had significant leadership authority and responsibility. I then followed with this: "If it is not about money or power, it must be that you just covet the title of Senior Pastor so much that you don't want to wait three years until you get it."

My successor was pretty quiet from that point on during "The Dinner." Instead of taking an aggressive posture, he withdrew. I saw his lack of response to my assertions as disrespectful. We left the restaurant with a potentially broken relationship. In the car on the way home, my wife shared her perspective, after I yelled at her for not being more vocal over dinner to agree with my assertions! She said, "Maybe his interest in accelerating the process is not about money or power. Maybe he just feels like it is time for him to spread his wings."

She reminded me that he had served at my side for almost fifteen years. She reminded me that he had agreed to be my emergency successor almost ten years earlier. She reminded me of my deep-seated conviction that he was God's choice to be my successor and the investment I had made in mentoring him to that end. She didn't have to remind me of the horror stories we both knew of pastoral succession plans that were destroyed by the way things were handled by the Senior Pastor. She settled me down, as she has done from time to time for almost fifty years.

I called my successor while we were still driving home, apologized to him and his wife for my defensiveness and anger, and set up a time to meet one on one to put a specific timeline and plan together. When all was said and done, the three-year plan turned into an eighteen-month plan. It was a plan that I became very much at peace with. With prayer and reflection, the intense emotions of defensiveness and anger dissipated much more quickly than I would have anticipated.

The Formal Handoff at Amplify Church

At Amplify Church's packed 2019 Good Friday service, I commissioned my successor in front of the congregation, pointing out his unique qualifications to take on the role. I read from Deuteronomy about the commissioning of Joshua that took place over three thousand years earlier, "The Lord said to Moses, 'Your time to die is near; call Joshua and present yourselves in the tent of meeting, so that I may commission him…' Then the Lord commissioned Joshua son of Nun and said, 'Be strong and bold, for you shall bring the Israelites into the land that I promised them; I will be with you.'" (Deuteronomy 31:14, 23) I assured the congregation that I was not about to die. Instead, I spoke about how much I believed in raising up next generation leaders and that the time was right.

I challenged each member of the church to think like Caleb. Caleb fulfilled God's destiny for his life under Moses' leadership and then he fulfilled God's destiny for his life under Joshua's leadership. The people of Amplify Church served God faithfully under my leadership and now they would do the same under my successor's leadership. Even though many of the people in the church were there because they had a strong connection to me, I encouraged them that "the best is yet to come."

I handed my successor a baton as a symbol of the transition—not a runner's baton but an orchestra leader's baton.

In an orchestra, every person has their unique instrument and gifts, just like the people of Amplify Church. The Senior Pastor is not called to play all the instruments but is called to unite the people of the church to create something beautiful. The symbol was meant to reinforce that Amplify was a church in which the Senior Pastor was all about maximizing the gifts and contributions of others. After my wife and I laid hands on and prayed for my successor and his wife, he spoke that night for the first time as Senior Pastor.

It was a bittersweet moment for me. I remember that night wondering, at least at moments, if I was doing the right thing, even though it was the culmination of a detailed eighteen-month plan. I still had a lot of energy. There was a strong sentiment in our church board of directors that I should stay in the role of Senior Pastor longer since things were going very well. Some felt that I should stay much longer. In addition, several friends and peers in ministry expressed concern. While thinking it was admirable that I was holding my role with open hands and that I was demonstrating my passion for investing in next generation leaders, it was also deemed by some to be premature.

And yet, despite any reservations, I also felt a strange peace. It was as if God was saying to me, "Mission accomplished." I had come to the church at the age of fifty with a God-inspired determination to restore the church's impact on our community and city. I also had a God-inspired determination to identify and mentor next generation leaders, including my successor, so that the church could continue to be a catalyst for transformation after I was gone.

To my surprise, I felt like a great weight was lifted from my shoulders that night. I later found out that my successor felt as though a great weight of responsibility was placed on his shoulders. It was.

I wish I would have modeled humility more effectively heading into the development of our detailed transition plan. Even though my season of defensiveness and anger was only a few weeks long, it could have led to a catastrophic relational break that would have negatively impacted the church in many ways. My pride almost caused everything I had worked for to unravel. And it all ended up being about moving my transition ahead by a mere eighteen months. After the transition, my successor organized a "Night of Gratitude," during which my wife and I were honored for our years of ministry at the church. It could have ended very differently.

I have been better at modeling humility since the transition took place. I have taken the role of prayerful cheerleader and have provided support without critique. Board members and church members know better than to send

> To my surprise, I felt like a great weight was lifted from my shoulders that night. I later found out that my successor felt as though a great weight of responsibility was placed on his shoulders. It was.

> Even though my season of defensiveness and anger was only a few weeks long, it could have led to a catastrophic relational break that would have negatively impacted the church in many ways.

me criticism about my successor or send him criticism about me. We both follow Terry Robert's advice: "Following the transfer, the veteran and successor should maintain a relationship of genuine affection and mutual respect, observable to the congregation."[54]

Amplify Church is my church for life. The congregation knows that I support him. Since the transition, I no longer attend staff meetings and board meetings, even though I have an open invitation. It is his turn to lead.

> "Following the transfer, the veteran and successor should maintain a relationship of genuine affection and mutual respect, observable to the congregation."

Something interesting happened that could not have happened if I had not moved up the timetable for my transition. A few months after the formal transition, I was recruited to serve as President of the Pittsburgh Leadership Foundation, the organization I referred to earlier in this chapter. It turned out to be the perfect fit for my education, my work and life experiences, and how God has wired me. That opportunity would not have been available had we stuck with my original pastoral transition timeline. My new season of ministry will leverage the wisdom I have gained over the years with more "breathing room" in my schedule and less stress in my life, which is a good thing. To me, it reinforces the truth that when we hand off one baton, God has another baton to put into our hand.

---

[54] Terry Roberts, *Passing the Baton: Planning for Pastoral Transition* (Coppell, TX: Independently Published, 2021), 69.

Modeling Humility—A Christ-Centered Reflection

It is common for pastors to want to stay in their role indefinitely, especially those who view themselves as indispensable heroes. One pastor in his late seventies who had no intention of handing off his role to a successor, said to me, "Certainly, God does not want me to me give up my position in the church and squander the wisdom I have acquired over the years." He didn't seem to realize that God could use his wisdom and experience even if he no longer held the title of Senior Pastor. Outgoing pastors need not fear that their next season of life will be unfulfilling. They need not fear that they can't have a meaningful ministry unless they hold onto their position. God's plan for us is bigger than that.

> Outgoing pastors need not fear that their next season of life will be unfulfilling. They need not fear that they can't have a meaningful ministry unless they hold onto their position. God's plan for us is bigger than that.

By the way, the indispensable hero syndrome is not just found in outgoing pastors. The Associate Pastor of one church was too impatient to wait until the time he had agreed he would be taking on the Senior Pastor role. He saw himself as the leader who should immediately replace the "old guy" and take the church to new heights. So he undermined the Senior Pastor with the staff, board members and church members. It backfired on him, and he ended up leaving not just church, but also leaving the ministry. Several disillusioned church members left as well. The Associate Pastor's pride and lack of integrity had a negative impact on the church, his ministry, and his family. He would have been wise to embrace the words of the only true Indispensable Hero, "Take my yoke upon you, and learn from me; for I am gentle and humble in heart, and you will find rest for your souls." (Matthew 11:29) For all Christ-followers, modeling humility should be seen as a virtue. For incoming pastors and outgoing pastors, modeling humility should be seen as imperative.

> *For your consideration: As you consider the reality that you will be transitioning leadership at some point, in what ways do you need to more effectively model humility?*

CHAPTER FIVE

Leadership Transition Pitfalls

When a man comes to this point in his life, he wants to turn over the things he's been blessed with to make sure that everything goes well after he's gone. You all know Michael Corleone and we all remember his father. At the time of my retirement or death, I turn over all my interests to his control.[55]

Hyman Roth

It was Roth who tried to kill me in my home. It was Roth all along. He acts like I'm his son, his successor, but he thinks he's going to live forever, and he wants me out.[56]

Michael Corleone

Leadership Succession is never easy. I am not aware of any pastoral transitions that involved hired killers as in *The Godfather: Part II*, but I am also not aware of any pastoral transitions that were perfectly smooth. Choosing Seamless Pastoral Transition certainly does not guarantee

---

[55] *The Godfather: Part II*, directed by Francis Ford Coppola (Hollywood: Paramount Pictures, 1974)

[56] *The Godfather: Part II*, directed by Francis Ford Coppola (Hollywood: Paramount Pictures, 1974)

success. Among the thousands of churches that have closed their doors in recent years, many were churches, no doubt, whose final pastor was installed after a Seamless Pastoral Transition.

The fact is, leadership transitions are fraught with pitfalls. That is why it is so important for church leaders to go into a pastoral transition with eyes wide open. I think of it this way. Not long ago, CNN covered the story of a man from Texas who went to a dock at Adams Bayou on the Texas-Louisiana border. One person told him as he walked onto the dock–"Don't go in the water, there are alligators in there." In fact, she told him that she had just seen a twelve-foot alligator with her own eyes. He heard that warning, and then looked at a sign with large letters–"NO SWIMMING – ALLIGATORS."

But even though he had a verbal warning and a written warning, he still started to remove his shirt as if he was about to go swimming. Another person nearby shouted, "Don't go in the water – there are alligators in there!" According to the news report, the guy shouted "BLANK the alligators!" and jumped into the water. Within seconds he was eaten by an alligator.[57] There is a lesson we can learn from this story: It is wise to avoid alligators.

There are plenty of alligators in the water during leadership transitions. I call them *Leadership Transition Pitfalls*. Out of the interviews I conducted for this book, along with

---

[57] Andreas Preuss, "Man mocks alligators, jumps in water and is killed in Texas," CNN.com, July 4, 2015, https://www.cnn.com/2015/07/04/us/texas-alligator-attack/index.html

insights from scripture and related literature, six specific pitfalls emerged. While it is certainly not an exhaustive list, these six leadership transition pitfalls are wise to avoid—Staying Too Long, Handing off the Baton Without Taking Another, Choosing a Clone, Failing to Address Financial Realities, Dismissing the Need For a Detailed Transition Plan and Trying to Undo the Transition.

Pitfall #1: Staying Too Long

Many outgoing pastors hold on to their office for just too long. They are like athletes who stay until their impact is so diminished that it hurts their team and compromises their legacy. Perhaps it is even harder for pastors to accept this diminished impact than it is for athletes since a pastor's "skills" are not physical.

The average age of the outgoing pastors in the churches whose stories are covered in this book was sixty-four years old (with the youngest being fifty-nine and the oldest being seventy-two). The average age of the incoming pastors was forty-four (with the youngest being thirty-eight and the oldest being forty-nine). The outgoing pastors recognized that the church would benefit from having a Lead Pastor who was decades younger—especially when it came to more effectively reaching the next generation. An aging Lead Pastor who hangs on too long often ends up leading an aging, declining church rather than a growing, multi-generational church. The right age to transition for each outgoing pastor will vary, of course. One thing is for certain—we all know stories of pastors who would have avoided a bad ending to their ministry if they had transitioned sooner.

None of the outgoing pastors I interviewed left because they believed they had "lost it." All were still passionate about the mission of their church and felt capable of continuing to lead. Yet each one chose to transition to a next generation leader, who had a different level of freshness of vision, openness to change, enthusiasm, energy and/or creativity. They left, pretty much, at the top of their game, understanding the reality of researcher David Kinnaman's words:

> Today the influences of technology, pop culture, media, entertainment, science, and an increasingly secular society are intensifying the differences between the generations. And many churches, leaders, and parents—the established generation—have a difficult time understanding these differences, much less relating to the values, beliefs, and assumptions that have spawned them. So we need younger leaders. Young leaders who speak the language of their peers are sorely needed because today's twentysomethings are not just slightly or incrementally different from previous generations.[58]

---

[58] David Kinnaman, *You Lost Me: Why Young Christians Are Leaving Church* (Grand Rapids: Baker, 2011), Loc. 53–54 of 437 (eBook).

In light of these realities, it is important for Lead Pastors to be proactive and not wait for others to bring up the topic of pastoral transition. Dr. Jay Passavant writes about the pastoral transition at his church and how important it was for him to initiate the conversation about that inevitable transition. He writes, "If the pastor fails to initiate this conversation, and if those in a position of authority, such as the board of elders, also fail to act, the process will begin with an undue and unnecessary amount of stress as a result. This is why it is so important that the Senior Pastor is the one to not only acknowledge that the time for change is approaching but to also be the one to lead and champion the change emotionally and spiritually. Ideally, this process should be embraced at least three years from the anticipated time of the succession event. When the Lead Pastor initiates the conversation, it provides a graceful invitation to others and lets them know that the topic is open for discussion."[59]

Rev. Dr. Jim Holley, who faithfully served for decades at historic Little Rock Baptist Church in Detroit, puts it this way, "In my spirit I felt like it was the time. You've got to be relevant for a new generation... I want to walk out. I don't want to be carried out. I have found a new person to take my place. I am looking forward to the transition. It is a tremendous opportunity to be able to participate in the future while I am here in the present... It's been a wonderful journey. I can look back and know I left a mark. But

---

[59] Jay Passavant. *Seamless Succession: Simplifying Church Leadership Transitions* (Orlando: Xulon Press, 2015), 24-25.

if you're not careful, you will fill the church and then stay too long and empty the church. I don't want to empty the church."[60]

It is not easy to take the courageous step of initiating a leadership transition because there are so many natural fears involved. But, as Brené Brown puts it, "At the heart of daring leadership is a deeply human truth that is rarely acknowl-

> "It's been a wonderful journey. I can look back and know I left a mark. But if you're not careful, you will fill the church and then stay too long and empty the church. I don't want to empty the church."

edged, especially at work: Courage and fear are not mutually exclusive. Most of us feel brave and afraid at the same time."[61] No matter how effective you have been as a pastor, your legacy will be determined, at least in part, by when and how you transitioned out of your role.

One common occurrence with the outgoing pastors in this study was that the congregation held a celebration to recognize their contributions. The outgoing pastor and his family felt honored at these events, where the gratitude for years and decades of service was genuinely expressed. I have seen a number of pastors who stayed too long, and left without such honor and, in some cases, left in dishonor. Don't stay too long.

---

[60] Reverend Dr. Jim Holley, "Pastoral Succession," *American Black Journal with Stephen Henderson* (Detroit, MI: Detroit Public TV on YouTube, Oct 26, 2021).

[61] Brené Brown, *Dare to Lead: Brave Work Tough Conversations. Whole Hearts.* (London: Vermilion, Penguin Random House, 2018), 10.

Pitfall #2: Handing off the Baton Without Taking Another

Marshall Goldsmith is a highly regarded executive coach who has worked with senior leaders in organizations world-wide. He made some interesting observations when facilitating a group of twenty-four CEOs who were all preparing to hand off leadership in their organizations to a successor, "All of the participants at our sessions realized how blessed they were and wanted to give back in their later years, make a positive contribution to the world, and leave a legacy. They wanted to help others in the same way that mentors, teachers, parents, and friends had helped them. Each person wanted to continue doing work that had true meaning. Instead of becoming a person who *used to be* making a difference, they all wanted to remain a person who *still was* making a difference."[62] In my experience, outgoing pastors still want to make a difference at least as much, if not more, than these outgoing CEOs. It could be said that pastors are wired by God to make a difference. That is why it is so problematic when an outgoing pastor hands off the baton of church leadership without identifying the new baton that God is handing to them.

Aerialists know before letting go of the trapeze, that another is arriving. That is what gives them the confidence to let go. Outgoing pastors who have not invested the time to prayerfully identify what they will be doing next are those least likely to really leave. An outgoing pastor

---

[62] Marshall Goldsmith. *Succession: Are You Ready?* (Boston: Harvard Business Press, 2009), 30.

in one of the churches in this study put it this way, "It is very important to be excited about what you will do next. That includes more time for family and hobbies, but it also needs to include making a substantial contribution in some new role."

Several of the outgoing pastors I interviewed moved into formal coaching roles. Their wisdom and experience proved to be invaluable to other church, business, non-profit and civic leaders. Others either created a new business or non-profit organization that was a good fit for their passions and gifts or became a leader in an existing business or non-profit organization. Ironically, two of the outgoing pastors I interviewed went through training to serve as interim pastors in congregations that did not (or could not) choose Seamless Pastoral Transition. Both found the role of interim pastor to be both meaningful and gratifying.

In his classic book, *Halftime*, Bob Buford writes about rejecting the notion that the second part of your life is destined to be a period of aging and decline, marked by the boredom that many retirees experience. He encourages leaders to use the "second half" to move from success to significance. He writes, "Augustine said that asking yourself the question of your own legacy—'What do I wish to be remembered for?'—is the beginning of adulthood."[63] In *Living the Life You Were Meant to Live*, Tom Paterson encourages outgoing leaders to ask God to help them to discover how to make the most of the coming years. He

---

[63] Bob Buford, *Half Time: Moving From Success to Significance* (Grand Rapids: Zondervan, 2015), 25,157.

writes, "One message that you should derive from an appraisal of your life is that we are to leave a legacy to the world. What you do is not solely for yourself. You were created not as an end point, but as a part of an unending plan of God. Legacy flows from what you determine will be the most meaningful contribution of your life."[64]

Carey Nieuwhof gives some practical advice about how to know where to invest your time, "You're probably passionate about the things you're gifted at, but passion can extend beyond gifting. The key to finding your passion is to look for things that give you energy. In other words, there are a handful of things you do that you find not only enjoyable but also energizing."[65] As you consider what you will be doing in the next season in your life, it is wise to consider, not only your God-given gifts but also the things you are passionate about.

> Many outgoing pastors experience a sense of loss without experiencing a sense of excitement about how God will use them in a new role. That is usually because the outgoing pastor waits until after leaving their role before spending the time and energy to prayerfully discern the next baton that they will be taking.

Many outgoing pastors experience a sense of loss without experiencing a sense of excitement about how God will use them in a new role. That is usually because the

---

[64] Tom Paterson, *Living the Life You Were Meant to Live* (Littleton, CO: Paterson Center, 2014), 244.

[65] Carey Nieuwhof, *At Your Best: How to Get Time, Energy & Priorities Working in Your Favor* (Colorado Springs: Waterbrook, Penguin Random House, 2021), 67,81-83.

outgoing pastor waits until after leaving their role before spending the time and energy to prayerfully discern the next baton that they will be taking. As one outgoing pastor put it, "Do not wait until the last minute to determine what is next!"

Pitfall #3: Choosing a Clone

It is tempting for an outgoing pastor to only consider a successor who is just like the outgoing pastor. After all, if they have been a good fit for their congregation, the best successor would be someone like them. It is unwise, though, to only consider a successor who is made in the image of the outgoing pastor. When David stepped up to face Goliath, Saul gave his approval with one caveat. Saul clothed David with his armor. But David said about Saul's armor, "'I cannot walk with these; for I am not used to them.' So David removed them. Then he took his staff in his hand, and chose five smooth stones from the wadi, and put them in his shepherd's bag, in the pouch; his sling was in his hand, and he drew near to the Philistine." (1 Samuel 17:39-40) David ended up doing just fine without Saul's armor.

Many outgoing pastors express a willingness to hand off leadership to a successor. But many also insist, as Saul did, that the one stepping into leadership does things a certain way. This is especially true when it comes to

> Many outgoing pastors express a willingness to hand off leadership to a successor. But many also insist, as Saul did, that the one stepping into leadership does things a certain way.

92

the style of preaching and teaching. The logic is that, if the congregation likes the outgoing pastor's preaching style, the incoming pastor must have the same style. In fact, the incoming pastor should be similar to the outgoing pastor in every way possible, with the exception of age—in other words, a younger version of self.

One of the most disheartening examples of this pitfall was at a church in which a planned succession was terminated over politics. Andy Stanley writes to both conservative and progressive church leaders, "When a local church becomes preoccupied with saving America at the expense of saving Americans, it has forsaken its mission."[66] The outgoing pastor would not have agreed with these words. He felt compelled to influence his church members to adopt conservative causes and vote exclusively for conservative candidates. The incoming pastor, who was loved and respected by the congregation, met with the outgoing pastor to express hope that the church might become less partisan so that people from more than one political perspective would feel welcome. The conversation did not go well. As a result of the incoming pastor not agreeing to the ongoing promotion of the outgoing pastor's political agenda, the succession plan was cancelled and the incoming pastor was terminated.

Rabbi David Baron reminds us, "Moses did not pick a less intense version of himself. Joshua was his own man, with an identity and style very different from that of Moses.

---

[66] Andy Stanley, *Not in It to Win It: Why Choosing Sides Sidelines the Church* (Grand Rapids: Zondervan, 2022), 13.

Moses was a prophet, nearly divine. Joshua was of the people, a warrior and natural optimist. Moses' great challenge was to teach his people to be nomadic. Joshua would have to wean them from the nomadic life and teach them how to settle the land. Moses had to inspire endurance and faith; Joshua would have to inspire his men to battle. Different skills for different times—Moses knew what his people would be facing, and selected a man who could keep them in touch with the old mission and sustain it in a new setting."[67] The desire for the incoming pastor to be a clone of the outgoing pastor is not a God-given desire.

An addendum to the topic of choosing a clone would logically include the discussion about choosing a family member as a successor. While any parent knows that children are seldom clones of their father or mother, it is natural to want to pass the baton on to a trusted family member, whether or not that person has the same leadership style as the outgoing pastor. My successor is also my wife's nephew. Though we were never close before I recruited him to join the staff of Amplify Church, we obviously became close over years of time working together. Given his calling to be a Youth Leader and Worship Director, he made an immediate and profound impact on our church and our ability to connect with the next generation. Over a period of fifteen years, his leadership capabilities were publicly validated time and time again in various roles, including starting an

---

[67] Rabbi David Baron, *Moses on Management: 50 Leadership Lessons from the Greatest Manager of All Time* (New York: Simon & Schuster, 1999), 204.

extension campus of the church that grew to several hundred attendees.

Many churches forbid relatives of a Lead Pastor from serving on the same church staff and/or becoming the Lead Pastor's successor. It is a logical restriction. Many such scenarios have gone wrong when sentiment for a family member becomes more important than a person's qualifications. Eli had his sons serving in the temple—even though they were unqualified and ungodly!

Joshua was not Moses's son. Solomon was, of course, David's son. There is no reason to believe that Elijah and Elisha were relatives. We know that the mothers of John the Baptist and Jesus were related. Paul clearly was a spiritual father who was mentoring Timothy for church leadership. If they were related in some way, would Paul have discounted Timothy's potential as a church leader in a church that Paul had founded? I don't think so—but who knows?

With any pastoral candidate, there are many issues to consider. With a relative, another issue must be considered. From my experience and observation, I would not recommend that a family member of the Lead Pastor be chosen as a successor. Nor would I discount the possibility that it could be God's plan.

Pitfall #4: Failing to Address Financial Realities

Unfortunately, many pastors stay too long in their roles because of financial issues. This is understandable because outgoing pastors in their sixties and older typically have the highest salary of their lives. As one pastor noted, "I am hesitant to voluntarily trade my steady salary for an uncertain financial future."

Even though they knew in their thirties, forties, and fifties that they should be investing in one or more retirement accounts, many pastors have procrastinated or severely underfunded those accounts. To complicate things even more, some pastors have opted out of Social Security so they do not even have that modest income to look forward to. They have preached for many years that God will provide, but they also have financial commitments to their families. A pastor in their early or mid-sixties has to consider how they will make things work financially for the next twenty or thirty years.

One advantage that pastors who serve in mainline denominations have is that they typically have a pension of some sort provided by their denomination. Perhaps this is one reason that pastors in mainline denominations seem to have less angst at the idea of passing on the baton to a new pastor. It is really difficult for pastors to objectively pray about the right time to let go if they have no pension or steady source of income.

It is important to note that mainline denominations, knowing that a pension is in place, tend to have clear restrictions on what a church can do financially for a retiring pastor. As one denominational executive put it, "We cannot allow a church to have financial obligations to a pastor who no longer serves the church." On the other hand, pastors of churches that do not belong to a denomination are dependent on their church board to come up with a fair arrangement. Terry Roberts contends that board members of churches without a pension arrangement should take this issue very seriously, especially for founding pastors or pastors with extended tenures. He writes, "There should be some kind of financial consideration for the veteran pastor. The nature of that consideration will depend on the circumstances of the transition and the church's financial ability. In some cases it may simply involve a generous, one-time gift. In others, it may involve continuing income after the transfer, especially if the veteran has a long history with the church, has been instrumental in the church's success, or will remain on the pastoral staff."[68]

In some cases, church boards have been quite generous. One church board determined that an outgoing pastor, who was also the founding pastor, would receive his full salary for the rest of his life. Another outgoing pastor, who was also the church's founding pastor, was provided half of his salary for life. To keep from burdening the church, his salary each year was limited to two percent of the church's previous year's income.

In some cases, church boards have not been as generous. One outgoing pastor who had served his non-denominational church for decades was given a one-time special offering of a few thousand dollars upon his retirement. After that, he was on his own. The outgoing pastor of

---

[68] Terry Roberts. *Passing the Baton: Planning for Pastoral Transition* (Coppell, TX: Independently Published, 2021), 63.

another church with no pension in place was gifted with a cruise that had an itinerary that the church board thought he would enjoy. After the cruise, the pastor had to figure out the rest.

Perhaps one of the most important roles of a church board is to ensure that a pastor is fairly compensated and can face life after retirement without financial fears. It is never too early in a pastor's tenure for a church board to confirm that the pastor has a long-term financial plan. As pastors enter their fifties, this discussion is critical, even if only with one or more people commissioned by the board. I actually think that many board members have acted in ways that grieve the Holy Spirit in their lack of proactive concern for the financial security of the pastor with whom God has blessed their church.

Yet ultimately, it is the pastor who must plan wisely. Andrew Flowers writes, "If you are a Senior Pastor, you have a huge responsibility to be a good steward of the resources that God has entrusted you. Not just the church's resources, but your own as well. Planning for the future means having a financial plan that will enable the church to afford the costs of succession, and it means having a personal financial plan that will provide for your needs when you leave."[69] A pastor should not stay in their role into their late sixties or seventies or eighties when a next generation leader would be more effective in advancing the mission of

---

[69] Andrew Flowers, *Leading Through Succession: Why Pastoral Leadership is the Key to a Healthy Transition* (Coppell, TX: Independently Published, 2017), 110.

their church. They definitely should not stay too long if it is primarily about their finances. Even if the board does not honor an outgoing pastor appropriately, pastors need not give in to the fear that God can't provide for them financially unless they hold on to the role of Lead Pastor.

> A pastor should not stay in their role into their late sixties or seventies or eighties when a next generation leader would be more effective in advancing the mission of their church. They definitely should not stay too long if it is primarily about their finances.

Pitfall #5: Dismissing the Need For a Detailed Transition Plan

Every pastor knows that it is highly unlikely that they will be in their role for the rest of their lives. As a result, many realize that it is a wise choice to select and mentor a successor. The problem comes when the details and timing of the transition are not determined and clearly understood. It is important to create a written plan that is accepted by the outgoing pastor, the incoming pastor, the church board, and, as needed the appropriate denominational executive. The details of that plan need not be shared with the congregation, but at some point, the congregation should be made aware of who the incoming pastor will be and when the transition will occur.

Everything can change when specific planning occurs. One Lead Pastor and those to whom he was accountable chose Seamless Pastoral Transition. While he was happy to name one of his Associate Pastors as his successor, he told that Associate Pastor that he was not permitted to share that information with others. As time went on, it became clear that the Lead Pastor, who was in his mid-seventies, had no intention of creating a plan with timing that would be communicated to others. The Associate Pastor, who was much loved by the members of the church, left out of frustration. The church suffered a decline that was tragically unnecessary.

It is easy to criticize this outgoing pastor, but the critic fails to realize the intensity of emotions that come when succession turns from a well-kept secret into a publicly shared detailed plan. Marshall Goldsmith points out one of the realities of leadership transition.

> One of the most common fears of CEOs who are getting ready to slow down and pass the baton of leadership is, 'If I announce my successor in advance, isn't there a danger that I will just become a lame duck? I certainly wouldn't want that to happen!' Almost every executive goes through this dialogue as part of the challenge of slowing down. This fear often results in postponement of the succession announcement until the last minute—and inhibits what could have been a much smoother transition process. When it is approaching time to leave, face reality—you *will* become a lame duck! Attention will shift to your successor. Her vision for the future

of the company will mean more than yours. If you disapprove of executive team members' ideas, they will just wait it out and resell the same ideas to your successor. People will start sucking up to her—in the same way they used to suck up to you. Make peace with being a lame duck—before it actually happens—and your life, your successor's life, and the lives of the executive team members will be a lot better.[70]

The idea of making a formal announcement to the church about succession can stir up deep emotions. Naming a succession date is even harder. That is why many succession plans are so nebulous. It keeps things in limbo and it ensures that everyone is afraid to ask the outgoing pastor about specifics.

No matter how intense the emotions involved, the outgoing pastor must take the initiative to create a written plan that includes a specific date for the handoff to the incoming pastor. Whether the length of

> No matter how intense the emotions involved, the outgoing pastor must take the initiative to create a written plan that includes a specific date for the handoff to the incoming pastor.

the plan is measured in months or years, a detailed "he must increase, but I must decrease" approach should be built into that plan. Ozier and Griffith refer to this time

---

[70] Marshall Goldsmith. *Succession: Are You Ready?* (Boston: Harvard Business Press, 2009), 11.

SEEMLESS PASTORAL TRANSITION

period as the Changeover Zone and write, "An extended, healthy timeline (from the decision to leave until a new pastor arrives) tends to be approximately eighteen months. Remember, there is 'preparation' even to get ready to enter the Changeover Zone. Often it can be helpful to time the transition so that the departing pastor leaves the church in the winter quarter (January-March), leaving time for the incoming pastor to lead the church through Holy Week."[71] How long before the outgoing pastor formally leaves their role should the congregation be made aware? The announcement of the date for the formal transition in the churches featured in this book was as short as six months and as long as two years, with the most common time-frame being the timeframe noted by Ozier and Griffith— approximately eighteen months. During that period of time, the incoming pastor takes on more and more Lead Pastor responsibilities.

The specifics of this handoff of responsibilities are best captured in writing. For instance, in an eighteen-month timeframe, the incoming pastor may preach twenty-five percent of the Sundays for the first nine months and fifty percent of the Sundays for the final nine months. In the months before the formal transition, the incoming pastor may be leading staff meetings and board meetings with the outgoing pastor present and supportive. Most staff members, church members and board members acknowledge that a planned, smooth transition is preferable to an "on/

---

[71] Jim Ozier and Jim Griffith, *The Changeover Zone: Successful Pastoral Transitions* (Nashville: Abingdon Press, 2016), 104, 106.

off switch" approach where one hundred percent of Lead Pastor responsibilities are held by the outgoing pastor until the date of the transition.

Pitfall #6: Trying to Undo the Transition

Perhaps there is no greater pitfall to Seamless Pastoral Transitions than the willingness of the outgoing pastor to return in order to "save" the church when the incoming pastor doesn't meet the

> Perhaps there is no greater pitfall to Seamless Pastoral Transitions than the willingness of the outgoing pastor to return in order to "save" the church when the incoming pastor doesn't meet the expectations of board members or church members.

expectations of board members or church members. The well-documented story of the failed Seamless Pastoral Succession at the Crystal Cathedral, a megachurch in Southern California, is a warning for outgoing pastors who are tempted to undo the transition. I visited that church on one occasion. The sanctuary and campus were remarkable. The church was crowded with people who definitely had a meaningful connection to the Lead Pastor, who was known worldwide due to his television ministry. When his successor was met with mixed reviews, he took back the helm of the church. Since his successor was also his son, the attempt to undo the transition devastated not just his church, which no longer exists, but also his family.[72]

---

[72] William Vanderbloemen and Warren Bird, *Next: Pastoral Succession That Works* (Grand Rapids: Baker, 2014), 101.

In his excellent book *Necessary Endings*, Henry Cloud writes, "Whether we like it or not, endings are a part of life. They are woven into the fabric of life itself, both when it goes well, and also when it doesn't. On the good side of life, for us to ever get to a new level, a new tomorrow, or the next step, *something* has to end. Life has seasons, stages, and phases. For there to be anything new, old things always have to end, and we have to let go of them."[73] Henry Cloud writes about a friend who observed, "Everything that I have that is of value has come from being willing to end something that I was doing and go to the next step. The endings and the great new beginnings are somehow linked together. You can't have one without the other. It is a weird paradox."[74] Yet, for any number of reasons, it is tempting for some outgoing pastors to try to undo their leadership transition. Perhaps they haven't clearly identified or taken hold of what God has for them in their next season. Perhaps they miss sharing the weekend messages and the admiration of those they inspired. Perhaps they miss the financial security that came from the Senior Pastor's salary.

It is no surprise that many traditions forbid any involvement of the outgoing pastor in the church they have left. Trish Greeves writes, "All mainline denominations have similar ethics pertaining to the relationship between pastors and congregations they previously served. These guidelines require the pastor to terminate all pastoral services,

---

[73] Dr. Henry Cloud, *Necessary Endings* (New York: Harper-Collins Publishers, 2010), 6.

[74] Dr. Henry Cloud, *Necessary Endings*, 230.

refrain from interfering in the life of the parish of the ministry of the successor, honor the record of one's predecessors and successors, and exercise caution regarding contact with former parishioners."[75] Yet, after significant research into the impact of these requirements, Greeves adds, "Every pastoral transition involves a unique history, present circumstances, and personalities. Although policies and procedures are essential for effective planning, administration, and training, they need to be thoughtfully, not blindly, applied."[76] Whether or not an outgoing pastor continues to attend the church they have been leading, they definitely should not spend time thinking about taking back their role—no matter how tempting it may be. It is the successor's turn.

What should an outgoing pastor do when their successor inevitably makes decisions and goes in directions that they don't agree with? If they care about their church, they won't join in with the critics. When they get calls with complaints, they won't listen with a sympathetic ear. Their job is now to be a prayerful cheerleader for their successor, something they would want to have if they were the successor! There is an old saying, "Do unto others . . ."

Not long ago, I was returning a rental car. After driving over the metal spikes, I noticed the sign that read, "Do not back up. Significant damage will occur." That is a good

---

[75] Trish Greeves, *Is "Stay Away" the Only Way? How Former Pastors Relate to Congregations They Previously Served* (Chapel Hill: Alban Weekly, Alban at Duke Divinity School, December 23, 2013), 2.

[76] Trish Greeves, *Is "Stay Away" the Only Way?*, 6.

image to keep in mind for outgoing pastors. If you have left your church in good standing, you can be certain that people will tell you how much you are missed. Some will tell you that you must come back for the good of the church. Board members, many of whom still feel more loyalty to you than they feel to your successor, will join the chorus. But outgoing pastors must not back up. Significant damage will occur.

Failure is Not an Option

P astoral transitions that go wrong can compromise the impact of any church. Too many churches have their mission put on hold—sometimes permanently—because of a failed pastoral transition. Barna's 2019 study on leadership transitions in churches contains sobering words.

> All things considered, pastoral succession is one of the most pressing issues in the Church today. How a church navigates a leadership transition impacts its ability to be effective on every other front: caring for those in need, providing theological instruction, confronting injustice, cultivating deep community, facilitating meaningful worship experiences and, ultimately drawing people to know and follow Christ. An unsuccessful or messy pastoral succession process can compromise these mission-critical efforts. On the other hand, a positive process of transition can propel a church into a new season of fruitfulness.[77]

---

[77] David Kinnaman, *Leadership Transitions: How Churches Navigate Pastoral Change – and Stay Healthy* (Grand Rapids: Baker Books, 2019), 10.

Considering what is at stake, prayerful preparation for pastoral transition must be one of the highest priorities for outgoing pastors, incoming pastors, denominational executives and church board members.

One church that navigated pastoral transition with full awareness of what was at stake was Allegheny Center Alliance Church (ACAC), a Christian & Missionary Alliance church which was established in the late 1800s. A pastoral transition at ACAC was seen as particularly challenging since the outgoing pastor, who had served the church for thirty-six years, was a legend in the church and in the urban community served by the church. However, as he approached his seventies, he felt deeply that the well-being of the church would be best served by transitioning the Lead Pastor role to a next generation leader. The outgoing pastor worked with the church elders to establish a succession planning committee to identify a successor and help to oversee the transition. The goal was to find a successor who had the leadership skills to ensure the continuity of the church's high impact ministry.

The incoming pastor, who was an external candidate, was prayerfully selected from approximately 100 applicants! He was given an opportunity to build "relational equity" with the church staff, board of elders, finance

> Considering what is at stake, prayerful preparation for pastoral transition must be one of the highest priorities for outgoing pastors, incoming pastors, denominational executives and church board members.

committee and congregation during a ten-month period when he and the outgoing pastor overlapped in their service to the church. It is interesting that the process to find the new Lead Pastor at Allegheny Center Alliance Church was named "Finding Joshua." As with the seamless leadership transition from Moses to Joshua, not one day went by during which the Lead Pastor role at ACAC was vacant, a key to the ability of the church to maintain continuity of mission and momentum.

The Critical Question

Each one of pastoral transitions highlighted in this book had unique challenges to address. Yet, each one was a success. By definition, *the measure of success for a Seamless Pastoral Transition is simply that the health and momentum of a church are not negatively impacted by an unnecessary gap in time between permanent pastors.* One key to these successes is that, in every situation, the outgoing pastor was involved in the process. The outgoing pastor was not an autocrat whose decisions went unquestioned. Rather, the outgoing pastor in each case was accountable to a bishop or other external authority and/or a church board or other internal authority. Every outgoing pastor worked together with the incoming pastor and, in several situations, a search committee. Each case study was an example of both community discernment and shared leadership.

> There is a critical question that every leader must ask—"Am I responsible for what happens after I leave my leadership role?"

There is a critical question that every leader must ask—"Am I responsible for what happens after I leave my leadership role?" Moses would have answered that question in the affirmative. He could not guarantee what would happen to the nation of Israel after his death, but he could make sure that the people were left with a proven, effective leader. The seamless leadership transition from Moses to Joshua averted a vacancy in leadership that could have been devastating for the nation of Israel. Ironically, the next generation of Israelites experienced that devastation when Joshua failed to do what Moses had done.

> After a while the people of Joshua's generation died, and the next generation did not know the Lord or any of the things he had done for Israel. The Lord had brought their ancestors out of Egypt, and they had worshiped him. But now the Israelites stopped worshiping the Lord and worshiped the idols of Baal and Astarte, as well as the idols of other gods from nearby nations. The Lord was so angry. (Judges 2:10–13 CEV)

Rayford Malone writes, "Jethro mentored Moses. Moses mentored Joshua. But who did Joshua mentor? In Joshua 24, we see Joshua has called all the tribes and their leaders to reconfirm their covenant to God and there seems to be one person missing—Joshua's protégé."[78] Joshua was an extraordinary leader but, for some reason, he did not identify and mentor a successor. The results were heartbreaking.

Derek Tidball writes, "While we get a picture of Joshua as a collaborative leader, we never get a picture of him as a mentor of a younger generation of leaders. He works well with his peers, but if he was committed to developing the next generation of leaders, the book that bears his name is remarkably silent about it. This is surprising in view of the close and beneficial mentoring he himself had received from Moses."[79] Terry Roberts adds, "How ironic that after serving as Moses' assistant and successor, Joshua died without a successor. Was this a factor in the spiritual failure of the next generation? To be sure, Joshua served his generation well. But is it possible that the next generation 'abandoned the Lord' because Joshua did not prepare a 'next generation' leader to step into his shoes? According to the book of Judges, after Joshua's death, there was no central leader and no cohesive, guiding vision to unite the people."[80] It is possible that

> "How ironic that after serving as Moses' assistant and successor, Joshua died without a successor. Was this a factor in the spiritual failure of the next generation?"

---

[78] Rayford E. Malone. *The Joshua Dilemma: Mentoring Servant Leaders to Transition Through Ministry Succession* (Dallas: Saint Paul Press, 2017), 81.

[79] Tidball, *Lead Like Joshua*, 157.

[80] Roberts, *Passing the Baton*, 23-24.

Malone, Tidball and Roberts are all being too hard on Joshua. It is also possible that they are not. There are so many things about Joshua that we should admire. But when it comes to leadership transition, don't be like Joshua.

During the time I was planning for my transition, I happened to visit the Space Center in Houston, Texas. I stood in the control room where five famous words were spoken during the Apollo 13 crisis in 1970 regarding the need to get Commander Jim Lovell and his crew back to earth safely after their moon landing had to be aborted. Flight Director Gene Kranz made it clear: "Failure is not an option."[81] I bought a coffee mug on which those exact words were printed as a reminder of the importance of applying those words to our upcoming pastoral transition. After a couple of times through the dishwasher, the words on the mug disappeared. Apparently, failure is an option.

Failure is always an option when it comes to leadership transitions. You cannot guarantee what will happen to your church under new leadership. But there are many things you can do that will be a blessing to your church when your tenure as pastor ends, including building your pastoral transition on a foundation of prayer. The prayer of Moses is a good place to start, "May the Lord, the God who gives breath to all living things, appoint someone over this community to go out and come in before them, one who will lead them out and bring them in, so the Lord's people will not be like sheep without a shepherd." (Num.

---

[81] Gene Kranz, *Failure is Not an Option: Mission Control From Mercury to Apollo 13 and Beyond.* (New York: Simon & Schuster, 2000), 12.

27:16-17 NLT) Then build on that foundation of prayer. Develop Leaders. Pave the Way. Model Humility. Avoid the classic pitfalls. I think that such actions are pleasing to God. I could be wrong, but I think it is possible that if you do everything you can for the well-being of the future of your church, you have a better chance of one day hearing the words, "Well done, good and faithful servant."

Works Cited

Adkins, Todd. *Pipeline: Succession at Every Level*. Nashville: LifeWay Christian Resources, 2017.

Anthony, Michael J. and Mick Boersma. *Moving on Moving Forward: A Guide For Pastors in Transition*. Grand Rapids: Zondervan, 2007.

Barna Group. *Trends in the Black Church: Celebrating Its Legacy and Investing in a Hopeful Future*. Ventura, CA: Barna Group, 2021.

Baron, Rabbi David. *Moses on Management: 50 Leadership Lessons from the Greatest Manager of All Time*. New York: Simon & Schuster, 1999.

Brown, Brené. *Dare to Lead: Brave Work Tough Conversations. Whole Hearts*. London: Vermilion, Penguin Random House, 2018.

Bucer, Martin. *Concerning The True Care of Souls*. Edinburgh, UK: The Banner of Truth Trust, 2009.

Buford, Bob. *Half Time: Moving From Success to Significance*. Grand Rapids: Zondervan, 2015.

Chang, Patricia M.Y. *Assessing the Clergy Supply in the 21st Century*. Durham: Duke Divinity School, 2004.

Chrysostom, John. *Six Books on the Priesthood*. Crestwood, New York: St. Vladimir's Seminary Press, 1996.

Cloud, Dr. Henry. *Necessary Endings*. New York, NY: Harper-Collins Publishers, 2010.

Cohen, Norman J. *Moses and the Journey to Leadership: Timeless Lessons of Effective Management from the Bible and Today's Leaders*. Woodstock, VT: Jewish Lights Publishing, 2007.

Colyer, Krystina. *Finance Team Building & Succession Planning Program Summary*. CFO Forum, August 6, 2019.

Coppola, Francis Ford, dir. *The Godfather: Part II*. Hollywood: Paramount Pictures, 1974.

Crabtree, J. Russel. *Transition Apparitions: Why Much of What We Know About Pastoral Transitions is Wrong*. St. Louis: Magi Press, 2015.

Crews, Joel. *Chick-fil-A Names Next CEO*. Kansas City: SOSLAND Publishing, MEAT+POULTRY, 9-17-2021.

David, Jerry W. and Steve Sells. *Honorable Design: The Art and the Order of Generational Transition*. Evington, VA: Brookstone Publishing Group, 2019.

Dingman, Robert W. *In Search of a Leader: The Complete Search Committee Guidebook*. Westlake Village, CA: Lakeside Books, 1994.

Dungy, Tony. *The Mentor Leader: Secrets to Building People and Teams That Win Consistently*, Tyndale House Publishers, Carol Stream, IL, 2010.

Dungy, Tony. *Quiet Strength: The Principles, Practices & Priorities of a Winning Life*, Carol Stream, IL: Tyndale, 2007.

Dungy, Tony. *Uncommon: Finding Your Path to Significance*, Carol Stream, IL: Tyndale, 2011.

Ferguson, Everett. *Ordination in the Ancient Church*. Restoration Quarterly 5, no. 3, 1961.

Flowers, Andrew. *Leading Through Succession: Why Pastoral Leadership is the Key to a Healthy Transition*. Coppell, TX: Independently Published, 2017.

Franc, Bradley J. *The Succession Solution: The Strategic Guide to Business Transition*. Coppell, TX: Woodview Publishing Company, 2019.

Godin, Seth. Seth's Blog, March 28, 2022, https://seths.blog/2022/03/re-calibrating/

Goldsmith, Marshall. *Succession: Are You Ready?* Boston: Harvard Business Press, 2009.

Greeves, Trish. *Is "Stay Away" the Only Way? How Former Pastors Relate to Congregations They Previously Served*. Chapel Hill: Alban Weekly, Alban at Duke Divinity School, December 23, 2013.

Haubert, Kathrine and Bobby Clinton. *The Joshua Portrait: A Study in Leadership Development, Leadership Transition, & Destiny Fulfillment*. Altadena, CA: Barnabas Publishers, 1990.

Heifetz, Ronald A. and Marty Linsky. *Leadership on the Line: Staying Alive through the Dangers of Leadership*. Boston: Harvard Business School Press, 2002.

Henderson, Jeff. *Know What You're FOR: A Growth Strategy for Work, An Even Better Strategy for Life*. Grand Rapids: Zondervan, 2019.

Holley, Rev. Dr. Jim. "Pastoral Succession." *American Black Journal with Stephen Henderson*. Detroit, MI: Detroit Public TV on YouTube, Oct 26, 2021.

Kinnaman, David. *Leadership Transitions: How Churches Navigate Pastoral Change – and Stay Healthy*. Grand Rapids: Baker, 2019.

Kinnaman, David. *You Lost Me: Why Young Christians Are Leaving Church*. Grand Rapids: Baker, 2011.

Kranz, Gene. *Failure is Not an Option: Mission Control From Mercury to Apollo 13 and Beyond*. New York: Simon & Schuster, 2000.

Kricher, Lee. *For a New Generation: A Practical Guide for Revitalizing Your Church*. Grand Rapids: Zondervan, 2016.

Malone, Rayford E. *The Joshua Dilemma: Mentoring Servant Leaders to Transition through Ministry Succession*. Dallas: Saint Paul Press, 2017.

Maxwell, John. *Developing the Leaders Around You: How to Help Others Reach Their Full Potential*, New York: HarperCollins Leadership, 1995.

Maxwell, John and Steven R. Covey. *The 21 Irrefutable Laws of Leadership*. Nashville: Thomas Nelson, 2007.

McLynn, Neil B. *Ambrose of Milan*. Berkeley: University of California Press, 1994.

Mead, Loren B. *Critical Moment of Ministry: A Change of Pastors*. Bethesda, MD: Alban Institute, 1986.

Mullins, Tom. *Passing the Leadership Baton: A Winning Transition Plan for Your Ministry*, Nashville: Thomas Nelson, 2015.

Neal, Stephanie, Jazmine Boatman and Bruce Watt. *Global Leadership Forecast*, Pittsburgh: Development Dimensions International, 2021.

Nieuwhof, Carey. *At Your Best: How to Get Time, Energy & Priorities Working in Your Favor*, Colorado Springs: Waterbrook, Penguin Random House, 2021.

Niewolny, Dean. *Trade Up: How to Move From Just Making Money to Making a Difference*, Grand Rapids: Baker Books, 2017.

Ozier, Jim and Jim Griffith. *The Changeover Zone: Successful Pastoral Transitions*. Nashville: Abingdon Press, 2016.

Passavant, Jay. *Seamless Succession: Simplifying Church Leadership Transitions*. Orlando: Xulon Press, 2015.

Paterson, Tom. *Living the Life You Were Meant to Live*, Littleton, CO: Paterson Center, 2014.

Preuss, Andrea. "Man mocks alligators, jumps in water and is killed in Texas." CNN.com. July 4, 2015. https://www.cnn.com/2015/07/04/us/texas-alligator-attack/index.html.

Roberts, Terry. *Passing the Baton: Planning for Pastoral Transition.* Coppell, TX: Independently Published, 2021.

Robinson, Anthony B. *Rethinking Interim Ministry.* Chapel Hill: Alban Weekly, Alban at Duke Divinity School, January 9, 2013.

Stanley, Andy. *Not in It to Win It: Why Choosing Sides Sidelines the Church.* Grand Rapids: Zondervan, 2022.

Strawn, Brent A. *The Old Testament is Dying: A Diagnosis and Recommended Treatment.* Grand Rapids: Baker Academic, 2017.

Tichy, Noel M. *The Leadership Engine: How Winning Companies Build Leaders at Every Level.* New York: HarperCollins, 1997.

Tidball, Derek. *Lead Like Joshua: Lessons For Today.* London: InterVarsity Press, 2017.

Time Magazine, *Religion: God & Steel in Pittsburgh.* New York: Time, Inc., March 21, 1955.

Vanderbloemen, William and Warren Bird. *Next: Pastoral Succession That Works.* Grand Rapids: Baker Books, 2014.

Volz, Carl A. "The Pastoral Office in the Early Church." *Word & World* 9, no. 4 (1989): 359-366.

Warren, Ben, *Chick-fil-A CEO Dan Cathy Steps Down*. Chicago: Mainland,1851 Franchise, 09/17/21.

Watkins, Ralph C. *Leading Your African American Church through Pastoral Transition*. Valley Forge, PA: Judson Press, 2010.

Weese, Carolyn and J. Russell Crabtree. *The Elephant in the Board Room: Speaking the Unspoken About Pastoral Transitions*. San Francisco: Jossey-Bass, 2004.

Woolfe, Lorin. *Leadership Secrets From the Bible*. New York: MJF Books, 2002.

Yoder, John. *The Schleitheim Confession*. Scottdale, PA: Herald Press, 1977.

CPSIA information can be obtained
at www.ICGtesting.com
Printed in the USA
BVHW051801170622
639936BV00002B/5

9 781662 851223